The British Papers

The British Papers

Acknowledgements

I would like to thank all the people who wrote an essay for *The British Papers* outlining their point of view about how our cities need to be planned in the future and for the experience they bring to this topic. I hope that now I have collected you all together, these papers can be drawn upon to gather people for various conferences in order to further inform others of our British expertise and the ways we can learn together to think about building a low carbon future. I would also like to thank Jess Mallalieu for helping put the pages together and RIBA Publishing for producing it. This idea originally came about with my colleague Angyla Wang in Beijing who wanted us to share our ideas on sustainable city -making.

by Angela Brady

Published by RIBA Publishing, part of RIBA Enterprises Ltd, 76 Portland Place, London, W1B 1NT

ISBN 978 1 85946 603 2

Stock code 85057

British Library Cataloguing-in-Publication Data
A catalogue record for this book is available from the British Library.

Production director: Kate MacKillop
Production controller: Michèle Woodger
Development editor: Sharon Hodgson
Copyeditor: Vicky Wilson
Printed and bound by CPI Group, UK

RIBA Publishing is part of RIBA Enterprises Ltd.
www.ribaenterprises.com

Contents

Foreword

Foreword

by Angela Brady PPRIBA

The British Papers is a collection of invited essays and opinions from architectural and urban-design leaders, as a snapshot of current thinking and approaches to sustainable city-making.

As President of the RIBA, I championed internationalising the institution to create new partnerships around the world, promoting British design expertise to encourage future collaboration.

During the heart of the recession, I led many RIBA, UKTI and British Council trade missions and spoke at more than a hundred venues in the UK, Europe, Middle East, US, China and Vietnam on the benefits of sustainable design and how we can work together on solutions that suit each other's history, culture and identity in the context of a responsible approach to the world's resources.

What promoted this outreach overseas began in 2004, when as chair of Women in Architecture we positively promoted diversity in our profession. We curated the DiverseCity architects' exhibition, which travelled to 34 cities around the world including the UK and Europe, the US, the Middle East, China, India and Australia. We invited each host city's architects to join the exhibition, showcasing their people and projects.

Thus the exhibition became known as the Global Snowball. From that time we experienced the benefits of sharing ideas and exchanging knowledge and appreciated the mutual respect shown for each other's culture.

During these visits it soon became apparent that in many developing countries, the mistakes of the west were being repeated. Soulless, rootless, gas-guzzling buildings were being put up without reference to their cultural context or suitability to local climatic conditions.

The UK is famous for innovation and design skills and the UKTI 'GREAT' campaign relays this message. One of the UK

▼ **Below:** *Angela Brady PPRIBA presented a talk with colleagues at the Ajman 2013 Urban Planning Conference. She is pictured here with the ruler of Ajman, Humaid bin Rashid Al Nuaimi*

highlights was our 2012 London Olympic and Paralympic Games. From procurement to legacy, we produced the most sustainable Games to date. We managed to capture the spirit of this achievement in our short film 'Designing for Champions'. Our campaign also filmed 55 key design voices during the course of the Paralympics.

As a way of influencing the sustainable-city debate I invited the authors of this collection of essays to share particular viewpoints about the latest design thinking. In this wide-ranging collection, English Heritage promotes regeneration via constructive conservation and the Academy of Urbanism discusses how our history, culture and identity anchor us in place and time.

Our top universities – the LSE, Manchester and Birmingham among others – are key to shaping our city-design thinking and creative architects and engineers pave the way with ideas and projects. There is research on Urban Agriculture from Brighton University and tree advice from Tree Design and Action Group.

This collection developed out of a collaborative project with my Beijing contacts from ten years ago, who requested a critical analysis of China's recent direction of development and asked for advice on how we could share sustainable knowledge. That set of essays was published in Chinese by Global Brand Insight in Beijing in 2014 as *The China Papers*.

With *The British Papers* we want to mirror that enthusiasm and welcome collaboration. I believe that the selected experts and professionals send a clear message about the great expertise and sensitivity to context we have here in the UK and the ways in which we can learn together to build better cities to help prepare for a low-carbon future.

Angela Brady PPRIBA

▼ *Below: Photograph taken during the 2012 London Paralympics and the making of the film 'Designing for Champions'. The film is now available on the RIBA website at www.architecture.com/Explore/Stories/DesigningforChampions.aspx. From left to right: John Nolan PPIstuctE, Peter Murray Chair NLA, Angela Brady PPRIBA and Kevin Owen ex LOCOG. London 2012 was the most sustainable Olympics and Paralympics to date*

Essays

An Integrated Planning and Design Strategy for Urbanising City Regions in China and Asia

by Professor Peter Head and Professor Laura Lee

Urbanisation has become the focus of Chinese governmental action at all levels, as signalled by the national government's introduction of policies regarding ecological civilisation since 2007 and the use of the term as a main policy goal during the Eighteenth Party Congress in 2012.

In parallel, the Chinese constitution has been changed to incorporate a 'Scientific Approach to Development' and 'Making Ecological Progress'.

It is recognised that a different mode of development is necessary for China, one that directs the majority of the increasing urban population to spaces that inherently reduce the consumption of energy and resources, help citizens into socially harmonious low-carbon lifestyles, and continue to offer opportunities to create jobs and to improve quality of life.

The development of such places, called eco-cities, is seen to be a necessity for China's sustainable development. However, eco-city planning has generally not taken real limitations on resources, economic feasibility, cultural history and social transformation into account.

The first attempt to do this was by Arup on the Dongtan eco-city planning project for Chongming Island in 2005–06, a project that did not get built. Since then, integrated planning and design has evolved substantially, as exemplified in Adelaide in Australia, and we now have evidence that this approach can support the demonstration and scale-up of transformational change in eco-city theory and practice in China. This paper aims to describe this approach and the new tools that are emerging to support it.

Professor Peter Head CBE
Structural Engineer
CEO, The Ecological Sequestration Trust
www.ecosequestrust.org

Professor Laura Lee
Architect
Adelaide Thinker In Residence 2009
www.thinkers.sa.gov.au/thinkers/lee

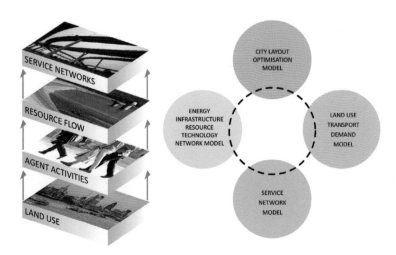

◀ **Left:** The benefit of integrated planning

The large-scale planning of a new city region moves through outline planning into a control plan and then into the phased delivery of infrastructure and buildings.

There will be certain social, environmental and economic objectives at the outset, reflecting the regional targets in the five-year plan – a 'sustainable development framework' – but quickly in many current planning processes the project tends to be broken down into a series of investments which are procured at least possible cost using local technical specifications.

Without an overarching integrated design strategy and systems model, the result of this phase of delivery is often to lose the social and environmental benefits as speed of delivery takes over, with teams working in sector silos.

With an integrated design strategy and systems modelling tools (for example, to relate resulting well-being and health to increased productivity and economic benefit), the creative design and delivery process leads step by step – through procurement that enables competition among designers and builders for the best performance outcomes – to delivery of greater value at lower cost.

The performance outcomes might typically include:
» Human and environmental health
» Economic vitality and individual prosperity
» Energy
» Housing
» Nutrition and urban–rural linkages
» Mobility and access
» Communications
» Education and culture
» Governance and civic engagement
» Water
» Materials and waste
» Ecological footprint

Multi-cultural, multi-skill teamworking

Integrated planning and design requires a different working approach. On Dongtan, much of the process was conducted through successive workshops with local stakeholders and the community. Workshops were held at least once a week in the early stages as designs were developed, with the largest such event including more than 90 people. A large number of different skills were required and almost everyone involved had to bring deep experience to enable the quick resolution of design matters.

Economists, engineers, ecologists, sociologists, architects, urban designers, financiers, business modellers, planners, utility and policy experts, art historians and archeologists all have very different ways of thinking. So the successful integration of convergent design development is a challenging process. It requires strong leadership and a deep understanding of how to carry out innovative design with a clear scope of work and a step-by-step set of deliverables.

Convergent sustainable-development masterplanning

It would be impossible to create masterplans quickly and efficiently to meet a complex set of objectives without a creative integrated planning platform that enables convergent sustainable-development value outcomes. These are called virtuous cycles of benefit that arise in city planning and they are learned from research and experience in cities all over the world.

For example, if people in the community are able to live and work close together and have access to good public services nearby, then they will travel less by car, so lowering emissions and improving air quality. This also lowers healthcare costs and improves both overall health and quality of life. This in turn makes the place cheaper and more desirable to live in and so demand goes up and the developer gets more development at a better price.

Integrated planning and design tools

A new opportunity is the use of computer-assisted modelling, simulation, monitoring and assessment methods, which can be adopted to supervise and measure the overall performance of city-development efforts and to support investment in new developments. This represents a new approach that pursues quantitative and qualitative improvements at all points in a city through scientific monitoring, recording and verification processes. These track the successes and setbacks of implemented hardware strategies – that is, strategies and technologies that improve the physical characteristics of land use, water, energy, waste and ecology regimes – as well as software strategies such as industry structuring, management, policies, standards and regulations.

The modelling can be applied in any well defined area to include all locally available 'resources' (non-renewable, renewable, already built infrastructure, people and ecology). The regional model contains all the relevant parameters, entities and transfers required for society and ecosystems to function, and for their interactions with the world outside the region through selected global models. The scale can accommodate at least 5 million agents.

Such a model will support the creation of a real-time model of human activity for 'smart' city-development investment as well as the feedback loops and information systems that will enable the population to make 'smart' lifestyle decisions. These tools can be configured to draw data directly from national databases such as earth-observation satellites, global climate models and underground geology databases as well as from local social and economic sources with appropriate layers of security.

Summary of the planning-performance objectives for a typical eco-city

Environmental protection

The city development will be separated from sensitive ecological areas by a buffer zone that will be both eco-park and wetland. Particulate-emission vehicles will be controlled so air quality will not deteriorate.

Battery-powered vehicles will be encouraged to lower both pollution and noise. Water will be captured and recycled within the city so current farmwater run-off containing nitrates will be greatly reduced. No waste landfill will take place on site as most waste will be recycled.

▼ **Below:** *Proposed harbour and fish market, Dongtan eco-city*

Biodiversity in the city will rise compared with surrounding farmland as areas of open water will increase, green roofs will attract more insects and urban parks will be planted with a rich diversity of plants and trees. There will be green corridors through the city.

Social and economic benefits

Business as usual would be, for example, a single-use housing estate on a 630-hectare site for around 50,000 people creating some 19,000 jobs. But the eco-city approach has 80,000 residents with 51,000 jobs, which means everyone who can work should find a job locally. Mixed-use development means jobs are located close by while social and retail services are clustered near three village centres. The developer is able to build twice as much floor space to sell than in the business-as-usual case and the place is more vibrant, healthy and attractive to live in.

Energy

The development runs on a high proportion of renewable energy with buildings designed so that energy demand will go down by 60 per cent compared with normal practice. Renewable energy will be produced using a combined heat and power plant, large- and small-scale wind turbines, photovoltaic panels on buildings, energy from the waste stream and groundsource heat pumps.

Water

Potable water derived from primary treatment and grey water recycled within the city will come from water stored in ponds and lakes. Separation of potable water together with good applicance design will enable consumption to be reduced while wastewater recycling will enable the discharge from site to be reduced by 80 per cent compared to normal practice.

Waste

All waste will be collected and most will be recycled into useful resources. Energy will be derived from biomass waste and minerals will be extracted and recycled into agricultural production.

Transport

Good public transport in the form of a bus/tram route will be available within 550 metres of all residential and commercial accommodation. A walking and cycling grid will cross the city and provide easy access for all, including disabled people. These routes will pass through parks and run alongside canals. Thus the use of cars will be discouraged and car trips will be shorter and fewer. Goods will all be delivered to a consolidation centre on the edge of the city from where they will be delivered street by street using zero-emission vehicles, rickshaws and watercraft.

Agricultural production

The aim is to create a level of food-production capacity in and adjacent to the city that is as great as on the farmland on which the city is built. This will take place partly in high-intensity food-production units in which high-quality green vegetables are grown, as well as on rooftops. Recycled nutrients and water will be used for this.

Implementation strategy and achievements in Adelaide

Adelaide, with 1.2 million people, has delivered an economically successful low-carbon transformation over the last ten years using integrated planning and design, with the following outcomes:

» Over 26 per cent of renewable electricity in the overall supply
» 120,000 PV roofs on 600,000 houses = 250 MW peak
» PV roofs on most public buildings
» Solar hot-water systems mandated for new buildings
» Three million trees planted on 2,000 hectares for CO_2 absorption and biodiversity
» 15 per cent reduction of CO_2 emissions since 2000
» Water-sensitive urban development
» 180,000 tonnes of compost made from urban organic waste
» 20,000 hectares of land near Adelaide used for vegetable and fruit crops
» Reclaimed waste water and urban compost used to cultivate this land
» Large-scale building tune-up programmes across the city region
» 60 per cent carbon-emissions reduction by municipal buildings
» Construction of Lochiel Park Solar Village with 106 eco-homes
» Thousands of new green jobs created.

The following additional implementation aspects are

helpful to support delivery of integrated design:

Collaborative construction capacity building has been effective through setting up a knowledge-sharing network, creating integrated construction processes and associated integrated technology research and innovation.

Manufacturing assemblies for mass customisation of buildings have been developed so that construction quality, high

performance and speed of construction go hand-in-hand.

Performance-based research alliances help build a library of successful case studies and share knowledge.

Design education and learning environments have been created in which integrated design is a core discipline to study at all levels from young children through to communities and mid-career staff.

▲ **Above:** *Proposed east village and health centre, Dongtan eco-city*

▼ **Below:** *Agent-based integrated planning and design platform*

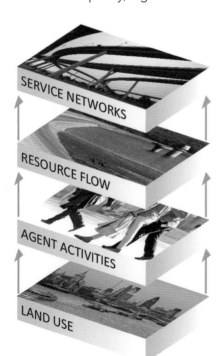

SERVICE NETWORKS

RESOURCE FLOW

AGENT ACTIVITIES

LAND USE

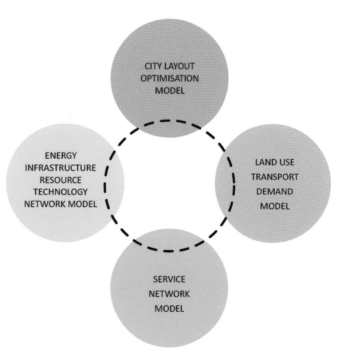

CITY LAYOUT OPTIMISATION MODEL

ENERGY INFRASTRUCTURE RESOURCE TECHNOLOGY NETWORK MODEL

LAND USE TRANSPORT DEMAND MODEL

SERVICE NETWORK MODEL

The Electric City

by Professor Ricky Burdett and Philipp Rode

Ricky Burdett
Professor of Urban Studies
Director, London School of Economics
Cities and Urban Age
www.lsecities.net

Philipp Rode
London School of Economics and
Political Science

As the visionary British architect Cedric Price noted over 40 years ago:

*Technology is the answer.
But what is the question?*

The notion of the Electric City offers a critical reflection on contemporary innovations in urban infrastructures and technologies as we become more aware of environmental challenges and the threats of climate change.

For over a decade our research at LSE Cities has focused on the relationship between the physical and social dimensions of cities. Increasingly, we are also turning our attention to the digital and ecological age, better to understand how its technologies and infrastructures are transforming our urban futures at both a social and environmental level.

Electricity shaped the architecture of cities at the turn of the last century. Arc lighting, elevators and trams revolutionised the urban landscape and the habits of many western cities as they expanded rapidly to absorb urban migrants. Electricity completely transformed cities and urban lifestyles, especially through public transport. In addition, the widespread introduction of petrol-based vehicles in cities of the post-World War II era led to a reconfiguration of the urban landscape.

Today electric power continues to fuel a massive expansion in the public utilities, transport, domestic appliances and modern commodities that characterise the 'urban age', where cities consume over 60 per cent of the world's energy and contribute to nearly 80 per cent of global CO_2 emissions.

Skyscrapers and suburbs, commuting and sprawl, ghettos and CBDs have all followed on from past waves of technological innovation. Cities have grown taller and fatter in the space of a few generations. Property values have gone up and slums have been created. Commuting times have escalated in some cities while others have rediscovered the efficiencies of the compact city, building on the synergies of increased proximity and more efficient public transport.

Today electricity is re-emerging as a common denominator of a new technological revolution as unprecedented advances in information and communication systems are matched by radical innovation in green-energy technologies and infrastructures.

Much of this pervasive innovation nexus of power

▶ *Overleaf:*

▶ *Top: Old modes of transport are reconnecting new inner cities (Tramlink, Croydon)*

▶ *Middle: Shared systems of mobility are changing urban dynamics (cycle hire docking station, London)*

▶ *Bottom left: Electricity has allowed buildings to be turned inside-out (Lloyd's of London)*

▶ *Bottom right: Canary Wharf at night*

and information is, and will continue to be, centred in cities. Smart grid technology and the internet of things, battery-powered vehicles and shared urban mobility, GPS-enabled apps for smart phones and integrated mobility services, online retail and virtual consumption, digital collaboration and e-governance are already part of our everyday urban experiences.

The more electricity generation is based on renewables – such as solar, wind and bio-fuels – the more electrification can deliver the greening of energy systems and cities. Electric mobility, electrically powered gadgets and systems, and even electric heating and cooling can help make cities more environmentally balanced, offering more than just cleaner energy. Today innovation can be found in both the public sector and private companies. Cities like Berlin, Paris and San Francisco have been proactive in leading this transition by combining e-mobility with car-sharing.

BMW, Peugeot and Toyota are re-inventing engineering paradigms for cars, concentrating on compact, light and energy-efficient electric vehicles as part of a multi-modal provision of mobility in cities. Utility companies are beginning to use electric vehicles to store renewable energy that needs to be taken off the grid during peak loads.

We use the term Electric City as a catch-phrase to capture

the social, economic, cultural and political complexities of what comes under the general banner of 'smart cities'. We recognise that these dimensions need to be better understood before new technologies are accepted by citizens who are highly sceptical of technological fixes and worried about affordability and data protection. At the same time, urban policymakers and city leaders seem hesitant to embrace change and impose untested technologies.

They are also concerned about the risks of investing at extremely high cost in what might turn out to be the 'wrong' technology. We hope that our research will stimulate debate and bring clarity, offering new insights into the social and environmental sustainability of cities.

London: the Compact City

by Richard Rogers KBE

Lord Rogers of Riverside
Architect
Rogers Stirk Harbour and Partners
www.rsh-p.com

Since the very first settlements some 6,000 years ago, cities have been created for people to meet and exchange ideas and goods. Cities are the engines of our economies and the greatest manifestation of a culture. They can brutalise or humanise people depending primarily on the quality of their design and the distribution of wealth within them. A compact, well connected, well designed, environmentally responsible, live-work-leisure city, where poor and rich can co-exist side by side and not in ghettos, is the only sustainable form of development, especially to help combat the greatest threat facing mankind – climate change.

Over the past 20 years, my city, London, has gone through a renaissance and today London and New York are *the* major global cities for culture and business. Yet 20 years ago Frankfurt was cited as the next business capital of Europe, something that seems difficult to comprehend today. In the 1980s London was haemorrhaging people, culture and confidence, and lacking both work opportunities and spaces that offered quality of life. Our degraded streets were not designed for walking and cycling, eroding the concept of the humanist and livable city. This is now changing

and I believe that in the next 20 years we will see cars banned from London's central boroughs, opening up even greater possibilities for public space and public life.

London's population has grown by more than 1 million people over the past two decades, and all indications are that it will have grown by another 2 million by 2033. It already has a housing crisis – the capital currently requires more than 800,000 new homes within the next eight years – so the addition of 2 million people will greatly increase the demand for homes and drive up prices, creating a greater divide between rich and poor.

Yet there are 3,600 hectares of unused brownfield land in the city – sufficient to meet all the housing needs of the foreseeable future, housing that will be close to existing transport hubs and infrastructure. Through well balanced and well designed development – with a mix of homes, offices, industry, shops and cultural activities – rundown areas can be redeveloped, repopulated and retrofitted, turning eyesores and empty sites into vibrant and dynamic communities.

Letting London continuously sprawl undermines its vitality and intensity. Sprawl increases

▼ *Below:* London's 600 localities

social fragmentation and damages environmental sustainability. To be rejuvenated, London's existing suburbs need to develop well balanced urban nuclei to create mini-centres or localities.

London is already a polycentric city made up of 32 boroughs, including 600 individual localities or areas [map 1, previous page]. This urban structure provides a particularly appropriate basis for a compact sustainable city. Each locality needs to have a focus for public life, with reinvigorated public spaces, civic amenities and opportunities for interaction between people, goods and ideas, developing the most appropriate model for the people it serves in a way that creates a distinct identity and character.

We must also reclaim London's 600 miles of local high streets; they are the obvious centres for sustainable growth [map 2, below]. These high streets need to be remodelled for greater public use, with buildings for health, leisure and learning, creating new opportunities for working and shopping locally. Reinvigorated high streets will form the heart of polycentres, major urban hubs that provide strategic services and opportunities as well as being strong employment and residential clusters.

London's green and public spaces should be linked to form a network of 'green grids' across the whole city [map 3, below right]. This 'green grid' will offer every citizen a bench near his or her front door, a tree as part of the view from his or her home, a park within a few minutes' walk as well as access to cycle networks and green routes stretching across the whole city.

If all this happens, we will have created a truly future-proofed city capable of responding to change and absorbing more people without detriment to the quality of its environment and its inhabitants' lives.

When planning our cities, we should be concerned with the social environment (and social inclusion) as well as the beauty of the physical environment. More than 2,400 years ago the young men of Athens (a world city at that time) had to swear an oath when they were formally inducted as citizens. The Ephebic Oath, as it was called, asked them to promise to 'leave this city not less but more beautiful than I found it'. This oath should be adopted by architects (and planners too), in the same way as doctors abide by the Hippocratic Oath.

Leaving a city more beautiful, more livable, more adapted to climate change and more equitable is surely the best legacy anyone can give to future generations.

▼ **Below (left):** London's 600 miles of high streets
▼ **Below (right):** London's green spaces

High-Speed Stations: a Catalyst for Economic Growth

by Sir Terry Farrell

Sir Terry Farrell
Architect
Terry Farrell & Partners
www.terryfarrell.co.uk

China's new high-speed line between Beijing and Guangzhou is over 1,428 miles long and reduces the journey from 22 hours to eight hours – a remarkable achievement. At both ends of this national line are integrated high-speed interchanges, designed by Farrells, which are considered to be world leading.

Guangzhou South is the largest railway station in Asia. It consists of 28 elevated island platforms for three national rail systems linking to three underground metro lines arranged with other transport modes over six floors.

At the other end is Beijing South, opened on time for the 2008 Beijing Olympics and a vital city-centre interchange with a projected annual passenger flow of 80 million in 2030.

Lessons for high-speed stations

Together, these stations show British design and transport expertise at its best and create new models for high-speed transport interchanges around the world.

Beijing South serves as a new gateway to the Chinese capital, with a catchment area of more than 270 million people. This fully integrated multimodal transportation hub is a major

urban and civic building – deliberately placed within the metropolis – as well as the centre of a masterplan for urban economic growth and development.

One of the largest contemporary railway stations in the world, it is designed for 286,500 passenger movements daily, and 105 million annually by 2030. To accommodate these vast numbers of people, a new model in railway-station design was developed, with a vertical separation strategy designed to make passenger flows direct, legible, convenient and highly efficient.

The level above the platforms is the Departure Level, housing waiting areas and ticketing facilities. The level below the platforms, the Arrivals Level, facilitates arriving passengers connecting to the metro

▼ *Below: Beijing South Station*

and other transportation modes. The station design is practical and functional, and follows a modern airport-terminal arrangement to accommodate the large number of passengers, reduce or eliminate cross-flows and assist with wayfinding.

A catalyst for new development

The new hub was located on existing railway land and one of the challenges was the way the geometry of the diagonal fan of the railway tracks sat within Beijing's cardinal urban grid. In response, the station acts as a gateway by inserting a landscaped pedestrian spine into Beijing's formal north–south axis as well as becoming a catalyst for new development within the surrounding urban area.

A number of the transportation facilities such as car parking, taxi pick-up and plant have been placed under the railway fan to minimise the footprint of the station. This naturally creates activity around it and energises the links to the surrounding areas, so it becomes an element joining up parts of the city rather than dividing it with inaccessible railway tracks.

The Chinese Ministry of Rail was able to take this clear, simple and people-oriented structure and utilise it as a model for China's future railway network. Used as a prototype and exemplar, the design has set a new precedent for stations in China. Through numerous design charrettes, the collaborative relationship ensured that the overall operational requirements were exceeded, with many of the features – such as the vertical separation of arrivals and departures at one end of the scale and the balustrades at the other – becoming part of the Ministry of Rail's system-wide station design.

▲ *Above:* Beijing South Station

Accommodating five levels with 11 island and two side platforms with 24 platform edges, interchange zones demanded an integral architectural solution to the complex requirements. The length of the new intercity trains helped determine platform size and operational requirements determined a platform length of 550 metres.

Incorporating sustainable technologies

The station was designed to reduce ongoing operational costs by incorporating sustainable technologies. A pilot project for building-integrated photovoltaics (BIPV) in China, the large oval roof was designed to cover the entire length of the platforms, to protect the station from the elements – sandstorms, cold harsh winters and extreme summer temperatures – and to moderate the indoor climate.

The catenary roof allows for unobstructed concourses, with large open spans offering light and airy spaces with generous ambient light and openness to reduce overcrowding, improve wayfinding and generate a feeling of safety.

Sustainable and environmental elements include natural cross-ventilation to reduce the cooling loads and air-binnacles to cool the Departure Level area, enhancing passenger comfort and at the same time reducing operational running costs.

With a construction site that was immense in size (1.5km long by 0.5km wide), contractors had to excavate more than 20 metres deep to accommodate the three metro lines.

▼ *Below (top): Beijing South Station*
▼ *Below (bottom): Kowloon Station*
▼ *Below (right): KK100, Shenzhen*

The project was co-designed with the local design institute, with engineering provided by Arup. China's Ministry of Rail's deputy chief engineer, Zheng Jian, said: 'Beijing South will be used as a benchmark because of its innovative architecture, energy-conservation features and its capacity to handle a peak passenger flow of 1 million people per day.'

Guangzhou South: catchment area 300 million

Guangzhou South, in contrast to the urban site of Beijing South, is set between two existing cities yet has the same transport-hub function with a catchment area of more than 300 million people.

It is the largest new station in Asia and includes 28 elevated island platforms (high-speed, intercity services and express) and three underground metro lines, arranged over six floors.

An elevated upper concourse is dedicated to departures; below this lie 28 elevated platforms. Beneath these platforms at ground level, city and station meet, with arriving passengers able to make connections to other modes of transport, including the metro and underground railway systems, which occupy the station's three subterranean levels.

Positive symbiosis between station and city

China's new high-speed service will eventually terminate in Hong Kong within the Kowloon station precinct.

This was masterplanned by Farrells in the 1990s and it now comprises a still-expanding transport super hub, with several million square metres of commercial air-rights development part funding the new transport network.

In another lesson for global infrastructure projects, many rail organisations are beginning to understand the value of development in and around their stations, and as at Kowloon are using them as a continuing revenue stream to finance rail operations.

▼ *Below: Guangzhou Station*

Public Transport TfL Sustainable Urban Design: Public Versus Private Transport

by Robin Buckle

Robin Buckle
Head of Urban Design Strategy
and Planning, Transport for London
www.tfl.gov.uk

With thanks to George Weeks, Urban Designer, TfL, in co-writing this paper.

The 2011 census revealed that London's population was 8.2 million and it is about to surpass 8.6 million, the highest it has been since 1939, rising to an anticipated 10 million by 2030. This is a growth of about 90,000 a year, or the equivalent of a full Tube train of people every three days. Economically, London now accounts for 22 per cent of UK GDP and it is the world's most visited city, with 16.9 million visitors in 2012.

When faced with figures such as these, it can be easy to forget that a city is more than numbers; it represents the combined interactions of millions of individual people. Every one of London's 8.6 million residents requires a city that is safe, healthy, convenient, accessible, prosperous and attractive. The extent to which these aims are achievable hinges on the ways people move around the city.

Since the turn of the millennium, there have been major changes in the way Londoners travel, largely guided by policies in the London Plan and the Mayor's Transport Strategy. There has been a shift away from private to public transport. Public transport's journey shares have risen from 34 per cent in 2000 to 43 per cent in 2011, while private motor transport's shares have fallen from 43 to 34 per cent. Cycling rates have doubled since 2001 and walking remains an important mode, accounting for just under a quarter of all trips.

This modal shift was enabled through investment in public transport, walking and cycling, and by charging drivers to enter central London. Public-transport provision has expanded, with 34 per cent more bus kilometres and 13 per cent more Underground kilometres since 2000.

Rail projects such as the London Overground have significantly improved connections in London's suburbs, while the roll-out of Oyster pay-as-you-go across Greater London has helped to make multi-modal journeys quicker and simpler.

Good public transport is of limited use, however, if the walking environment is poor. During any journey a person will spend some time as a pedestrian. The public realm must therefore be good enough to integrate public-transport provision into the urban fabric and of sufficient quality to provide a timeless and seamless interface between those elements of the fabric it connects.

Land is a precious resource in a city; allocation of land purely to motor traffic means it is unable to fulfil any other function. The central London congestion charge was introduced in 2003 to reduce traffic and congestion; any net revenue from the charge must, by law, be used to improve transport. The scheme has reduced the number of vehicles entering the congestion-charge zone by around 60,000 per day.

This, along with the introduction of a Low Emission Zone (LEZ) for heavy vehicles, has helped reduce PM_{10}, NOX and NO_2 pollution. London aims to bring about a 60 per cent fall in CO_2 emissions from 1990 levels by 2025 – this is addressed in the Mayor's Climate Change Mitigation and Energy Strategy.

Faced with a rapidly growing population, London is continuing to invest in public-transport infrastructure. The £14.9 billion Crossrail project includes 42 kilometres of new tunnels and will increase rail capacity by 10 per cent. A public-realm improvement programme will ensure that the pedestrian environment at Crossrail stations is conducive

to onward travel by foot or bicycle.

Cycling continues to grow in importance. The Mayor's Vision for Cycling in London, published in March 2013, further increased the bicycle's presence in the transport landscape. This complements the introduction of the Barclays Cycle Hire scheme in 2010, which has broadened the appeal of cycling and made it easier for people to access bikes, particularly for short journeys. Also, the TfL Business Plan to 2021 includes a cycling budget of almost £1 billion, unprecedented in London and UK terms.

One area where many of these changes can be seen is the Vauxhall Nine Elms Battersea Opportunity Area. This is rapidly changing from a low-density, car-based industrial area to a high-density residential and commercial neighbourhood, based on walking, cycling and

public transport. A £1 billion extension to the Northern Line is being designed to ensure that the area has high levels of accessibility by public transport. Nine Elms Lane, the main road, was designed for industrial uses and heavy vehicle traffic but is being reinvented as a tree-lined boulevard, with wide pavements, attractive street furniture and an ambition for segregated cycle lanes. This will link the new Underground stations with the surrounding developments via high-quality public space and demonstrate that this is now a place for people.

The changes taking place here are in some ways a microcosm of London. High-quality public transport, coupled with investment in a people-friendly urban realm, will lead to a city that provides a higher quality of life, is better for the environment, more energy efficient and a pleasure to live in, work in or visit.

The Queen Elizabeth Olympic Park: Promoting Sustainable Lifestyles

By Kathryn Firth

Kathryn Firth
Chief of Design,
London Olympic Legacy
www.queenelizabetholympicpark.
co.uk

We are building new neighbourhoods on the Queen Elizabeth Olympic Park that will enable communities to live sustainable lifestyles by integrating low-carbon, resilient infrastructure into the Park.

Residents who move into our new neighbourhoods will not have to worry about servicing their boilers as there will not be boilers in their homes – they will instead be connected to a low-carbon, park-wide district heat network that is more efficient and less carbon intense than individual gas boilers.

Their homes will be accessible, adaptable and highly energy efficient, built to standards designed to enable homes to be zero carbon. Our new residents can also expect to be using much less energy to warm their homes than the London-wide average.

They will be able to see the energy they are using via smart meters and so be able to reduce their consumption even further.

Residents on the Park will also benefit from fantastic public-transport infrastructure with each new home being no more than 350 metres from a bus stop, thereby reducing air-polluting road congestion.

Pavements and pedestrian routes are generous and our roads will be cycle- and pedestrian-friendly, promoting more active forms of transport. Homes that have on-plot parking will be supplied with electrical charging points to encourage the use of non air-

▼ **Below:** Queen Elizabeth Olympic Park looking north along WaterWorks River, flanked by the Olympic Stadium, the Orbit and the Aquatics Centre

polluting modes of transport All homes, whether houses or flats, are provided with space for secure cycle storage and a cycle-hire scheme will be extended into the Park. With respect to 'green' networks, Queen Elizabeth Olympic Park provides a missing piece of the 'jigsaw' of strategic open spaces defined by the East London Green Grid. The Green Grid will create a network of green spaces that connect with town centres, public transport nodes, the countryside in the urban fringe, the Thames and major employment and residential areas.

The potential benefit to London's economy is significant climate change through promoting walking, cycling and accessibility,

reducing environmental risks to make more sustainable business locations and shape and support growth more generally.

The green spaces of the Park, therefore, build upon the ecological setting of the Lea Valley and have been designed into the fabric of our new communities, ensuring that our residents are able to benefit from richly biodiverse public spaces that will help reduce the risk of surface flooding and also prevent our streets from overheating during the summer months.

Biodiversity is further fostered through the integration of green and brown roofs which will be irrigated by rainwater harvesting where possible.

Efficient water usage is an important aspect of both the sporting venues on the Park and the new neighbourhoods.

With respect to the former, non-potable water is used for all toilets. Homes will enable low water use through low-flow fittings and appliances, achieving 105 litres per day per person as compared to the current London average of 144 litres per day per person.

In summary, every effort has been made to integrate sustainability into the parklands, public realm and buildings that will comprise this new piece of city situated where the 2012 London Olympic and Paralympic Games – the greenest Games ever – took place.

INSIDE A HOME

EFFICIENT APPLIANCES
Highly efficient appliances help to reduce energy usage.

LOOK SMART
Smart meters are standard to help you monitor and control your energy use, and allow you to fit smart appliances.

WASTE NOT
Indoor and outdoor space is provided to store waste and recycling, and to encourage composting of organic waste.

USING EVERY DROP
Roofs and gardens are irrigated by water from rainwater harvesting. Low flow showers in the bathroom help you have a great shower using less water.

COOL COLOURS
The light colours of the buildings reflect the sun's rays and keep your home cooler. The whole-of-life impact of materials selection is always considered.

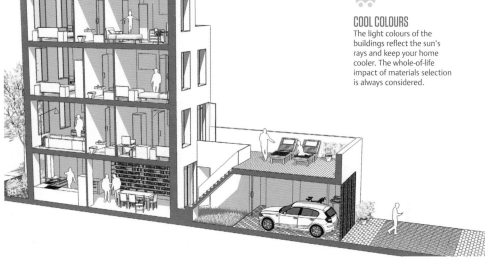

◄ *Left:* '*Inside a Home*' - *excerpt from the LLDC publication* Your Sustainability Guide to the Queen Elizabeth Olympic Park 2030 (*April 2012*)

Sustainable Urban Design and UK Specialism

by Thomas Bender

Thomas Bender
Lead Advisor for Design Review,
Design Council / CABE
www.designcouncil.org.uk

Design Review is a tried and tested method of promoting good design and a well-established way to improve quality and add value to schemes. The process seeks to improve the quality of the built environment for the public good and focuses on ensuring that places better meet the needs of the people who use them.

Cabe's Design Review traces its history back to the establishment of the Royal Fine Art Commission in 1924. Design Review is an independent and impartial evaluation process, where a panel of built-environment professionals assesses the design of development projects.

Our panel includes architects, landscape architects, planners, engineers, sustainability specialists, artists and academics. Over the past 15 years alone we have design reviewed more than 3,000 schemes, which means our experienced team are well placed to share best practice and help those using the service to achieve the best possible designs. The UK government acknowledges the importance of Design Review and it is now a key part of the planning process. Design Review brings direct benefits to the many different groups involved in the planning process.

Design teams and clients are given access to feedback and critiques from a panel of their peers at key stages of the design process. By supporting good design intentions, Design Review provides a fresh, external view that can identify issues the project designers may be too close to see. It offers constructive, impartial advice from fellow professionals to help project designers to assess their work from a broader perspective and identify any fundamental weaknesses.

This model of design support has been applied successfully across England and Cabe at Design Council has advised on a diverse range of high-

▼ *Below (left): The chair of the Design Review summarises the comments made by the panel on the design quality of the proposal*

▼ *Below (middle): The panel undertakes a site visit in order to understand and appreciate the impact of the proposal on key views along the River Thames*

▼ *Below (right): Two panel members have a closer look at a model to analyse the concept behind the elevational treatment*

profile projects including London towers such as The Shard, power stations and large infrastructure buildings, urban masterplans, hospitals and retail schemes. Specialist panels worked on Crossrail, on the new government-promoted series of eco-towns and on the renewal programme for secondary schools, 'Building Schools for the Future'.

In addition to the buildings, the space between them is equally important. So we also review landscape-design proposals for parks and squares. Every scheme that comes to a Design Review is scrutinised in terms of the quality and amount of public space it provides. Given the increasing density of the proposals, safeguarding decent spaces for recreation and leisure activities is a key aspect of our work.

One of the great successes of Design Review is our recent involvement in the London 2012 Olympics. We worked with the Olympic Delivery Authority from an early stage, training its team and advising on everything from project planning and procurement to building design.

Ambitions for the Olympic Park always stretched far beyond its immediate purpose. The vision

was to regenerate a deprived part of London, and the magnitude of the challenge was matched only by its potential for lasting change.

Our panel commented on the design quality of the sports venues, sponsor pavilions, restaurants and landscape design, and ensured that the Queen Elizabeth Olympic Park looked stunning for athletes, fans and the global television audience.

Most importantly, the panel considered the legacy aspects of the Park and how this formerly deprived area of London could be transformed into a new thriving and sustainable community. The huge success of the Park has permanently changed the way the construction industry thinks about design. And the fact that it was completed on time, to budget and to a high standard has enhanced the worldwide reputation of the UK's design and construction industries.

Another new major London intervention is the Thames Tideway Tunnel, a 20-mile 'super sewer' that will extend the existing outdated sewerage system and reduce the outflow of sewage into the Thames. The works, currently planned for 24 sites across

▲ Above: A site model is used to assess the relationship of the proposal to its immediate urban context in a review of a key site that will be highly visible from the river

▲ Above (left): Panel chair and panel members discuss the design quality of the proposal

London, include a number of proposals for new or upgraded public spaces that will be available for Londoners to use once the tunnel is completed.

Our Design Review service has provided an arena for Thames Water, local authorities and statutory agencies to consider how good design can help address key project challenges, not least by promoting the benefits Londoners stand to gain from this monumental engineering feat, which rivals the great public works of past centuries.

Some sites are in the centre of the historic capital, which makes it even more important to ensure that they are sensitive to context and fulfil their potential to provide new public spaces. Thames Tideway Tunnel's recognition of this has helped us to identify the shared challenges and opportunities associated with each site. There is the potential for a celebratory design that adopts a confident, rather than apologetic, relationship with its surroundings.

Constructive Conservation: English Heritage's Approach

by Carol Pyrah

Carol Pyrah
Planning and Conservation Director,
North East, English Heritage
www.english-heritage.org.uk

*In April 2015 English Heritage became **Historic England**, a government service championing England's heritage and giving expert, constructive advice, and **English Heritage**, a charity caring for the National Heritage Collection of more than 400 historic properties and their collections.*

www.HistoricEngland.org.uk

Wherever we are in the world, mankind has influenced the landscape. Whether creating beauty or desolation, our effects on the places around us represent a huge investment of time, physical resources, money and human endeavour. It is only natural that we should want to conserve the best we have of our human past, celebrating the creativity and talent of our forebears and learning from both their mistakes and their successes.

In 2013 in England we celebrated 100 years since the introduction of the 1913 Ancient Monuments Act, a law which recognised the state's duty to protect the physical remains of the nation's history. In the course of that century, our outlook on protecting the past has evolved into a positive and collaborative approach to the active management of change.

Fundamentally, the 'constructive conservation' practised by English Heritage (the government's statutory advisor on the historic environment) ensures that important historic sites and buildings have an ongoing value and use in the future. It uses historic places to help create jobs, expand businesses, and sustain economic prosperity and quality of life.

Thirty-six examples across the country are showcased in *Constructive Conservation: Sustainable Growth for Historic Places*. At the heart of this are English Heritage's *Conservation Principles, Policies and Guidance for the Sustainable Management of the Historic Environment*. (Both are available at www.english-heritage.org.uk/publications.)

By identifying why or how a historic site or place is important, we can pinpoint opportunities for change. Starting from a good understanding of what it is that makes a building or place special, English Heritage works in partnership with owners, developers, local authorities, architects and engineers as part of a multi-disciplinary problem-solving team.

St Pancras International – the rail gateway to England from Europe – is a highly visible example of the way that heritage-led conservation can be an engine for growth. The magnificent train shed of 1865–68 is Grade I listed – the highest UK heritage protection. Its length has been doubled for Eurostar trains, and a second station added for domestic travel.

Giant openings in the original train deck allow the previously unseen undercroft to be used as a new arrivals and departures area, with a substantial shopping and restaurant complex for travellers. English Heritage worked closely with the design team and the local council over a ten-year construction period. The result is a fittingly impressive welcome to England's capital city.

At the other end of the scale is Dewar's Lane Granary in Berwick-upon-Tweed, on the English–Scottish border. This six-storey former granary on the medieval quay walls had not been used since 1985 and many thought the only answer was demolition.

But the Berwick-upon-Tweed Preservation Trust (an independent charity set up by local people to save the town's heritage) took on the challenge of finding a new use for the building, and raised over £5 million for its restoration.

With radical modern intervention, the former granary is now a flourishing youth hostel, restaurant and high-specification art gallery. It has restored life to the surrounding streets, helping other local businesses to grow and succeed.

Constructive conservation is an inherently sustainable activity because it re-exploits the energy already invested in a building's construction – a far more efficient strategy than demolition followed by new build. English Heritage supports innovative schemes that protect and enhance the significance of buildings and places.

Our experience shows that modernising and reusing historic buildings is good for business, good for economic growth, and good for the quality of life of present and future generations. With creativity, passion and confidence, monuments from the past can continue to change and live, providing homes, jobs and activities for centuries to come.

▼ **Below (left):** *Before conversion – Dewar's Lane Granary, Berwick-upon-Tweed*

▼ **Below (top):** *After conversion – Dewar's Lane Granary, newly opened youth hostel, bistro and art gallery*

▼ **Below (bottom):** *St Pancras International Station, London*

History, Culture and Identity

by Steven Bee

Steven Bee
Chairman, Academy of Urbanism
www.academyofurbanism.org.uk

The principles of good architecture set down by Vitruvius around 15BCE in *De Architectura* – 'firmness, commodity and delight' – remain sound foundations on which to base urban design. Those responsible for commissioning and designing new buildings and spaces know how to make them look good and work efficiently. That may not, however, be sufficient to create a great *place*. For this, the Academy of Urbanism adds a further principle – vitality.

It is the way space is occupied that brings it to life, and it is the quality of urban life that the Academy of Urbanism aims to understand better, to encourage and to celebrate. The Academy's annual Urbanism Awards have now recognised 135 great places of all sizes. These are all places that have evolved over time,

sometimes millennia. This is reflected in their buildings and spaces, in their cultural institutions and demographic diversity. All display a distinctiveness that is valued by their inhabitants and visitors alike.

Our assessments of these places have identified some common characteristics:

Time-depth
Historic places that demonstrate the greatest vitality are those which have been able to adjust to and accommodate changing needs, expectations, activities and standards over long periods. This is reflected in the evidence of sequential development that provides a rich urban experience.

The lesson for urban designers is that beautiful buildings and spaces must be capable

▼ **Below:** *The vibrant streets of Lisbon in Portugal have adapted and changed over many years*

of adaptation if they are to maintain their qualities. This requires both sound construction with good materials and flexible layouts than can be changed without losing the inherent character of the place.

Examples: Lisbon, Copenhagen, Bordeaux, Jewellery Quarter Birmingham and Lace Market Nottingham.

Stewardship
Places with a long history have enabled institutions, companies and authorities to establish a long-term view of their investment. The returns come from revenue rather than capital receipts.

This perspective encourages the slow and steady growth of a community, of businesses, of cultural activities and of amenities. These in turn tend to be diverse and resilient to external pressures and competition. Such places

tend to be both confident and stable.

As NLA puts it following recent research into the Great Estates of London: 'Much of the story of London's development can be traced through the historic ownership of large pieces of land which, through the on-going ownership of freehold assets and their lease terms, have created a resilient cycle of change and renewal. Today this long-term attitude to investment, development and management has influenced the development of new large-scale and mixed-use areas, such as King's Cross, Canary Wharf and the Queen Elizabeth Olympic Park.'

The lesson for developers is that long-term investment in property ownership is likely to secure the long-term social and economic well-being of an area, and that over time this can provide a better return than realising capital growth.

▲ **Above:** *Jewellery Quarter, Birmingham, which mixes heritage and new uses*

Examples: Lamb's Conduit Street, Regent Street and Coin Street London, and The Royal Mile Edinburgh.

Leadership
Many historic places have succeeded through the efforts of a particular individual or organisation. The most constructive form of leadership draws its strength from popular endorsement. This is different from the simple exercising of power. Many historic places are the result of an assertion of power in ways that modern principles of equality would not support. Sustained progress today requires leadership across a wide range of interests.

Some places struggle because they have too many leaders. Co-operation, sharing and a willingness to modify individual aspirations to support public interests will focus energy and enthusiasm and avoid wasted effort.

Examples: Barcelona, Kings Place London, Freiburg.

Adaptability
Physical layouts that can be modified without compromising historic features are more easily adaptable to changing needs and expectations. They can accommodate and encourage

innovation and ensure continuing economic success and cultural vitality.

Examples: King's Cross Central and Clerkenwell London, Antwerp.

Distinctiveness
Distinctiveness derives from the particular features of a place. Its location and historic circumstances result in a range of buildings, spaces and activities that is unique.

Local distinctiveness cannot be designed-in, and attempts to import distinctiveness from elsewhere generally fail.

The design of new buildings and spaces should reinforce the distinctiveness of a place and not exploit or dilute it.

Examples: Steep Hill Lincoln, Bordeaux waterfront, HafenCity Hamburg, Derry Londonderry.

Vitality
The primary aim of those responsible for designing and investing in new places and those responsible for managing and regenerating existing ones should be the quality of life they encourage. The historic places that people value most are those which attract economic, social and cultural activity. The design of places should encourage the interplay between these activities, and their mutual reinforcement.

Examples: Saltaire Bradford, Merchant City and Buchanan Street Glasgow.

▲ **Above:** *The gradient of Lincoln's Steep Hill, together with its offer of individual retailers and historic buildings, creates a distinct setting*

▼ **Below:** *Freiburg, Germany. The city is internationally renowned for its sustainable and strong leadership*

▶ **Overleaf:** *Birmingham's Jewellery Quarter*

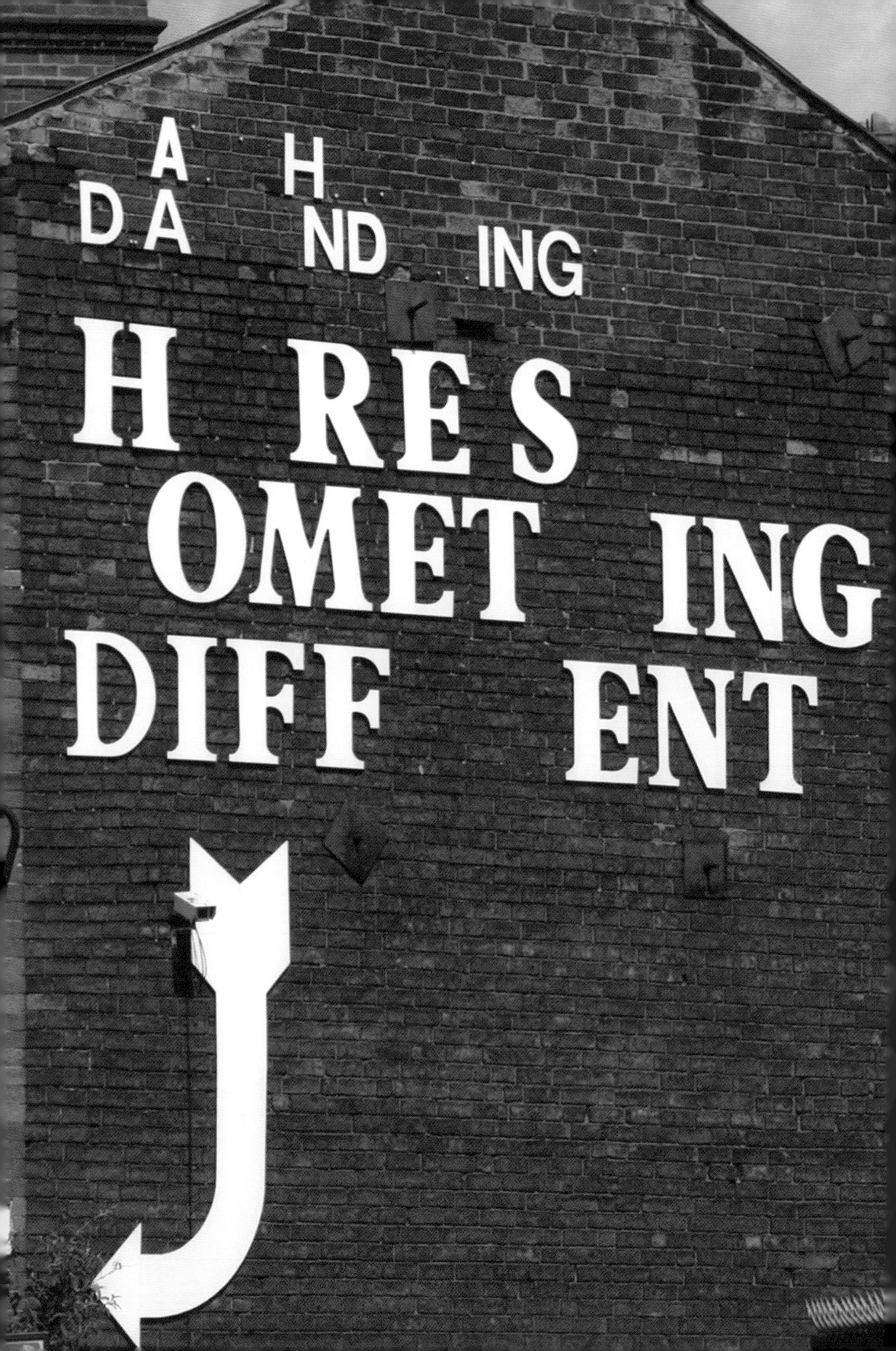
A H
DA ND ING
H RES
OMET ING
DIFF ENT

What Is Green Design?

by Dr Ken Yeang

Dr Ken Yeang
Ecoarchitect
www.kenyeang.com

For the architect, the compelling question is how do we design for a sustainable future? We need to understand and to address by design the environmental consequences of architecture's functions and processes, finding new design models, seeking new construction and production systems, developing green materials, assemblies and processes, and determining what actions we need to take to realise this vision.

The design profession has a key role to play in bringing about this transformation. Environmental issues such as climate change and pollution are also architectural problems, in as much as the bulk of our emissions and landfill waste comes from buildings. Green design must become the core value for all architecture, changing the way we design. But what might this look like in practice?

Green design starts with us, the human species and the most powerful species on the planet. Humankind will not stop consuming, stop employing land for its activities, stop producing things, stop using the products of our industrial systems, stop building or stop constructing infrastructures. Yet we must start to reduce our demands on the environment and its natural resources, to reduce our exorbitant levels of consumption (away from society's present 'consumer culture') by eliminating a wasteful way of life and lowering overblown standards of living and comfort.

Our human society has to change its existent polluting industries, unsustainable economies and commerce, and methods of production. To become sustainable, we need to radically alter how we live, build, behave, work, make, eat, learn, buy and move about, all of which affects our building requirements. The less we need means the less we build, and the lower the demand on the environment.

We shall be mistaken if we regard green design as just about engineering. Engineering systems, whether eco-engineering or cleantech, are of course important components of green design, giving us expediency of support for human society's habitation, ways of life, environmental enclosure and comfort, and other aspects that make our lives pleasurable. While engineering technologies are rapidly advancing towards ever greener and cleaner solutions for our built environment, it must be clear that eco-engineering is not the only consideration within green design.

Neither is green design just about rating and accreditation systems such as LEED, BREEAM or carbon profiling. These certainly provide useful guidelines but they are not comprehensive. Rather, they function as checklists or reminders of key items to consider and are useful for comparing buildings and masterplans using a common standard.

Clearly green design has now entered the mainstream of architecture. Virtually every architect, planner and designer today lays claim to practise green design – though some, of course, are greener than others. In effect, there are 'shades of greening' within design. Achieving complete green design involves much more than simply complying with the above systems; it is not as easy as has been contended and our sphere of knowledge needs to increase greatly before we become ecologically literate.

We might define green design as the seamless and benign environmental biointegration of everything we make (the synthetic and artificial, artefacts and built systems) with the natural environment and all that we do within it. The context for our human and built environment is nature or the biosphere, which is home to all living organisms and natural systems. We need to be aware that nature is an exceedingly complex and interdependent set of items, where the many parts,

whether biological or physical (geological, etc.) are held in intricate and delicate balance. Our ignorance about how and why this all works greatly exceeds our knowledge.

The start of the present environmental devastation came with the onslaught of industrialisation in the 20th century, which produced

a multitude of benefits for humankind but had correspondingly negative impacts on the natural environment. While the natural environment and natural systems have some resilience to tolerate gross impairments from time to time and can in local instances recover, they

▼ *Below: Editt Tower, Singapore*

cannot endure these impacts forever.

We contend that it is this failure to successfully biointegrate that is the root cause of our environmental problems. If we were able to biointegrate all our business and industrial processes, all our built systems and everything we do or make within our built environment (which includes buildings, facilities, infrastructure, products, refrigerators, toys, and so on) with the natural environment in a seamless and benign way, there would be no environmental problems whatsoever.

Successfully achieving this, of course, is easier said than done, but herein lies the challenge.

We can draw an analogy here between ecodesign and prosthetic design in surgery. A medical prosthetic (whether an artificial arm, leg or organ) has to physically and systemically biointegrate with its host, the human body. Failure to do so successfully will have negative consequences for both.

By analogy, this is what ecodesign must achieve: a total biointegration of our human-made built environment and activities with our organic host – the planet's natural environment – in a benign and contributive way. Ecodesign is thus design that successfully biointegrates our artificial systems both mechanically and organically with the host system of the biosphere.

▼ *Below:* Chongqing, China

Prototyping Innovation and New Systems for Sustainable Architecture

by Bill Dunster OBE

Bill Dunster OBE
Architect
Principal, ZEDfactory
www.zedfactory.com

In almost any country, the construction industry tries to resist environmental innovation. It is always cheaper to invest in strategies that have already achieved economies of scale and so provide the developer with cost certainty. The same applies to urban design, with many cities simply pressing the cut and paste button on planning applications, potentially resulting in excessive replication.

This is particularly devastating when development models from one country are applied in a different cultural context and climatic zone many years after the original has been discredited. For example, high-rise residential surrounded by urban freeways and island parkland without easy pedestrian access is a model frequently applied in China today but which has been banned in most of the west for decades. We are valuable because we recognise the mistakes we have made in the UK.

Testing new urban morphologies and prototyping construction systems with a lower carbon footprint is of massive benefit to the government since this reduces funds spent on the import of fossil fuels as well as air pollution and urban gridlock.

Politicians need to be given confidence that the hard work involved in lobbying for higher environmental performance standards is going to pay back by improving the standard of living of the majority.

The Beijing Ministry of Housing has world-class leadership through the office of Qiu Baoxing, and the current informed and rigorous strategy planning within the Chinese urbanisation programme is probably the best we have ever seen. A pattern of controlled and monitored low-carbon innovation can only be delivered by building demonstration best-practice projects to test new ideas. Working with the best international consultants and the brightest universities

▼ *Below: BedZED, South London*

allows the delivery of new urban quarters that challenge the existing orthodoxy and demonstrate that a higher quality of life can be achieved with fewer resources and a lower carbon footprint.

For instance, the London ZEDfactory-designed BedZED in south London demonstrated to the UK government that it could fit all of the 3.6 million new homes needed at the time on existing stocks of brownfield land while giving each home a garden and south-facing conservatory. Integrated solar energy would meet a meaningful percentage of thermal and electric demand at a density of around 120 homes per hectare.

This project and others gave the UK government the confidence to create the Code for Sustainable Homes, which provided a roadmap to achieving zero-carbon status by 2016. This London case study also won a competition set by the Shanghai city government for the best-practice demonstration area at the World Expo 2010. It was adapted and built in under six months to show how

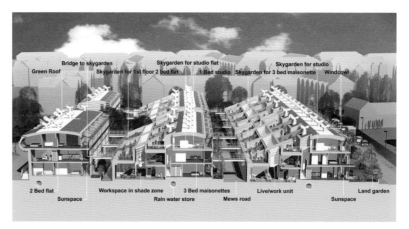

▲ *Above: BedZED, South London*

traditional Chinese live / work typologies could become zero carbon.

A similar project for the Dalian government shows how China could build alternatives to high-rise residential while matching identical densities and retaining the small-scale allotments and local farming practices that often get trampled by urban expansion.

Finally, ZEDfactory has been working with some of the best Chinese component manufacturers to create products that reduce the cost of building low- and zero-carbon projects for both domestic use and export. For instance, by redesigning the aluminium frame around a solar electric panel to become

a waterproof joint, the cost of a traditional roof can be used to subsidise a renewable energy installation, providing a beautiful dappled light to the space below. This product is being in manufactured for Milton Keynes in the UK and Zhangwu in China.

With a grid-connected feed-in tariff coming fast in China, these first projects will provide valuable information that could transform the construction industry and provide international leadership, with China now having the potential to set the highest environmental standards and reap the trade benefits.

▼ *Below: Dalian, China*

Sustainable Urban Design
by Chris Wilkinson OBE

Chris Wilkinson OBE
Principal Architect
WilkinsonEyre Architects Ltd
www.wilkinsoneyre.com

WilkinsonEyre Architects takes sustainable design extremely seriously and all our projects are audited by our in-house sustainable-working panel. We try to attain the highest standards of sustainability within our built work, incorporating fresh approaches that result from innovative thinking. Through our work on The Crystal in London for Siemens and the Gardens by the Bay for NParks in Singapore we have explored building-energy solutions and have achieved self-sufficiency in both cases.

The Crystal, designed in conjunction with Arup, is clad almost entirely in glass and has a programme that traditionally requires high-energy use including an exhibition and conference centre and offices. Yet it meets its energy requirements in a sustainable way.

The main features are rooftop photovoltaics, which generate 50 per cent of the peak-time electrical output; 17 kilometres of geothermal piles to supply all the building's heating and the majority of cooling; mixed-mode ventilation with openable windows; extensive monitoring and control systems with thousands of sensors feeding information to the BMS (building maintenance system); and black water harvesting. This is combined with an extremely sophisticated façade design that uses six different types of glazing to maximise efficiency.

Our Gardens by the Bay project had a brief to explore 'climate change' by replicating both a Mediterranean and a cool high-altitude climate in a tropical setting. This was achieved in two huge cooled glass houses without using energy from the mains grid.

▼ **Below:** *Gardens by the Bay, Singapore*

In collaboration with environmental consultants Atelier 10, a highly sustainable solution was found, using clippings from the trees in the landscaped public areas as biomass fuel to fire the energy system. This natural material, collected by the National Parks Board, would previously have been dumped as waste, so to use it in a positive way makes it doubly sustainable. All water falling on the site is collected, recycled and purified by the plants in the gardens, helping to establish self-sufficiency.

Our Guangzhou International Finance Center is a high-rise mixed development of office, conference, retail and serviced apartments with a gross floor area of 380,000 square metres. Designed with Arup, it was the winnning entry to an international competition held by the city planners in 2008 to provide a landmark for the Zhujiang New Town site. It was completed in 2011.

The tower was part of a strategic masterplan to consolidate a new civic centre that would replace the overcrowded, gridlocked and polluted old town. The new centre contains a major public extension to the metro system, several cultural buildings including an opera house, as well as many high-rise commercial and residential buildings.

Guangzhou, which is China's third city, is the heart of one of the country's most important industrial regions. It is known as the Garden City because of its abundance of planting but it has been suffering from serious pollution as a by-product of the factories that encircle it and its heavy car use.

Clearly the introduction of new public transport systems will help to ease traffic congestion and many more metro lines are needed. By comparison, Beijing is completing one or two new metro lines per year, which is barely keeping up with demand. Here we have been involved in the design of new stations such as Lize, where a transport hub will provide the focus of a new central business district.

Building tall, as with the 103-storey Guangzhou International Finance Center, makes sense for cities with huge predicted growth. Such high-density development reduces the uncontrolled expansion of city centres but needs to be complemented by sustainable public transport and balanced by sufficient public open space.

▼ *Below:* Guangzhou International Finance Center, China

Nigel **Eckersall**

Towards a Low-Carbon Design for the Middle East

by Nigel Eckersall

Researching low-carbon design solutions has been one of our chief priorities throughout our projects in the Middle East, notably in Qatar and the UAE. But rather than look to technology to solve the age-old problem of cooling buildings and streets in a hot climate, we studied the culture and identity of local cities. Our research demonstrated that the formation of these cities was derived from the need to survive in the arid environment, and that this had generated natural low-carbon and passive-design solutions.

It was by studying the unique characteristics of the architecture of the Middle East that we discovered that vernacular buildings in the area's cities were designed as part of an intrinsic cooling system. Each building was set in an architectural relationship to the others or to the 'lay of the land' to create natural cooling currents through basic principles of physics and fluid dynamics.

Ancient man knew not only not to walk in the heat of the sun, but also how to make a small opening on the shaded side of a building to create a powerful breeze, an unrecorded skill that was almost lost in the appetite to design modern cities for the oil-boom economies.

Research has revealed that the combination of the hot desert winds and cool easterly sides of buildings helped create natural cross-flows. When combined with water features, these produced cooling to the quality of modern electric air-conditioning systems.

Using this groundwork, we then set out to tackle the challenge of how to create

Nigel Eckersall
Architect
Partner, NSE Architects
www.nsearchitects.com

▼ *Below: Traditional techniques using water and air currents are harnessed to provide solutions to cooling the Qatar 2022 FIFA World Cup stadium*

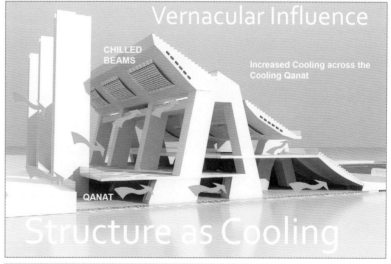

a low-carbon design for the world's most energy-consuming event, the Qatar 2022 FIFA World Cup. Strict criteria set by FIFA demanded we achieve a wet-bulb globe temperature (WBGT) of 26 degrees Celsius at the kick-off spot. A WBGT temperature reading also has to take into account humidity and wind speed.

Our solution was to create a stadium that used the following design fundamentals of ancient Arabic cities:
1. *Hot wind deviation and cool wind generation* through creating a Venturi effect in narrow alleys between buildings.
2. *Qanat water cooling* to reduce humidity and create accelerated air currents.
3. *Badgheers*, which is the use of cross-flows of hot wind into the architecture to create cool winds through internal spaces.
4. *Thermal mass* to absorb the winds' high air temperatures and so create cooled winds.

The result was an 80,000-seat stadium that achieves 24 degrees WBGT on the terraces and pitch. The design

envelops the stadium in an architectural skin with carefully placed openings to allow hot winds to enter between the layers. These winds are then directed downwards towards a qanat.

The qanat cooling system is an ancient method of creating cool winds by passing hot air across water chambers (qanats). The qanat for the stadium takes advantage of the constant need for de-watering the site and the fact that the water removed has a natural temperature of 14 degrees. When the hot winds are directed across the cooler water, their temperature is reduced to the necessary 24 degrees with a humidity ratio of 50 per cent.

The structure was designed in modular form to be constructed off site. It is made up of hollow tubes that take the structural load and act as HVAC ducts to deliver the cooled winds directly to the terraces and edges of the pitch. The velocity of these winds is set at 12 metres per second with a reach of 40 linear metres. During the hot

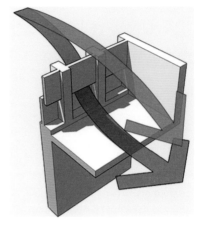

▲ *Above: Air-flow diagram*

summer months in Qatar, the wind is regular, and as temperatures increase, air speed also increases, so increasing the level of cooling.

We are now developing ways of creating water through natural cooling systems to provide water to parts of the world that have arid spells in the summer months.

We believe that such systems are a vital part of creating truly sustainable low-carbon cities for both the present and future.

▼ *Below: Qatar 2022 FIFA World Cup stadium*

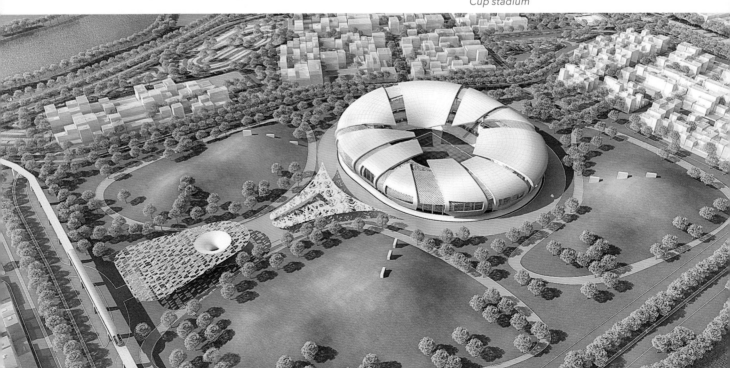

Does the manic pace of construction leave enough time and space for critical thinking?

by Angela Brady PPRIBA

Angela Brady PPRIBA, Architect Director, Brady Mallalieu Architects Past President , Royal Institute of British Architects www.bradymallalieu.com

A large part of my time as President of the RIBA was spent visiting cities around the world, in particular in rapidly modernising areas such as China, Vietnam and the Middle East, where I have seen at first hand the frantic and reckless rush towards modernity that is occurring. Through my own architectural practice, Brady Mallalieu Architects, I have been involved in the development of city-scale projects in China and have had to work within the challenging short delivery spans allowed for design teams to produce their work. I have seen the way 'off the shelf' western-style buildings are duplicated around the world, creating identikit cities that reproduce the planning errors made during our own rush for modernity in the 1960s and 1970s. I have seen the wholesale destruction of old and historic buildings and neighbourhoods and watched areas of cities developed over a thousand years flattened in a week to be replaced by nondescript, gas-guzzling glass tower blocks that were out of date before they were even built.

Despite our growing knowledge and the widespread acceptance of the reality of climate change, the lethal effects of carbon emissions on global temperature rise and the health issues created by smog and atmospheric pollution, most new buildings still follow an architectural and technological model developed in the west in the middle of the last century, well before such issues had any influence on current design standards.

Within this challenging scenario I have also seen many wonderful and inspiring projects developed with insightful clients, which dare to be different by using low-carbon design solutions that look towards a brighter, more humane future.

All of this continues on a scale almost unimaginable from a western perspective. In looking for pointers within it all, I would make four observations:

1 History, culture and identity

Many fast-developing countries do not seem to value their own history, culture or identity. Western models of architecture and urban design are regarded as desirable, aspirational and 'the future'. Older neighbourhoods and historic buildings are not just considered out of date, but are seen as standing in the way of progress and profit. We have been there ourselves in the UK.

▼ **Below:** *Chongqing New North Zone, public exhibition model*

The conservation movement developed gradually over a lengthy period following the 1960s and 1970s, when many towns and cities were needlessly ripped apart and many historical buildings

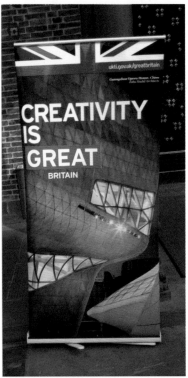

sacrificed to a crude vision of modernity. The backlash, when it came, was not from architects and developers but from the general public – from people helpless to prevent the destruction of their home towns, people losing their identity and the backdrop to their lives and seeing it replaced by alien and unsympathetic buildings that profited only their creators.

This popular revolt has now ensured that historic context and sense of place are properly considered in development projects in the UK and our towns and cities are richer and more humane places as a result.

◄ *Left: A Creative Sector Taskforce was set up by UK Trade & Investment (UKTI) to help creative businesses win high-value contracts overseas*

▼ *Below: Brady Mallalieu's proposal for a mid-rise Chinese city centre with streets at roof level and large courtyards*

Beijing needs its hutongs and Ho Chi Minh City needs its wetlands. Too often layers of history are scraped away to rid sites of 'old stuff' that supposedly no one cares for, obliterating the memory and history of whole populations along with the stories that made their places special. Too many pages have been ripped from our history books.

2 Time and space for critical thinking

The timescales for the construction of major projects and indeed whole new cities are driven by profit and political expediency. This does not serve the process of city-building well and does not leave space for consideration and critical thinking. The relentless pace can kill innovation and force designers to fall back on stock solutions, leading to the proliferation of identikit, car-dominated,

unsustainable cities. The speed of delivery insisted on in many developing countries, and particularly in China, is a major obstacle in the path of progress towards a more relevant and better model for 21st-century urban planning.

A second consequence of this is the personal toll on the people striving to meet these timescales. At our own practice Brady Mallalieu Architects, we have experienced this at first hand. Our colleagues in China surrender their family lives to an almost 24/7 working regime and similar effort is expected of western consultants. That can't be good for anyone or for the long-term future of the project. Designers of construction projects

▶ **Right:** *Developers Msheireb are transforming the centre of Doha, recreating a sustainable way of living rooted in Qatari culture*

▼ **Below:** *Tall towers in Dubai, many of them empty*

that affect the quality of so many lives must be given the time for critical thinking and time to learn from previous projects so there is continuous improvement in the way places are designed.

3 Technology appropriate to climate

In hotter climates from Baghdad to Marrakech, thousands of years of traditional Arab building techniques kept people cool naturally, shaded by

tall, narrow, walled streets and aided by wind- and water-cooling techniques. But since the arrival of the oil age the international air-conditioned glass tower block has entirely supplanted this native technology, so now in many parts of the world it is normal practice to travel between buildings in air-conditioned cars, as the roads are too hot and social expectations and lifestyles have changed. Now we are starting to look beyond the oil

age and traditional solutions to environmental control are coming back into focus, informing a contemporary architecture that learns from and reinterprets relevant traditional technologies, to create context-led solutions that are appropriate to specific climates, environments and available natural resources.

4 Local initiative for integrated design

To popularise and promote this approach to site-specific rather than universal urban solutions, I suggest that Regional Design Centres of Excellence could be established in major or second-tier cites undergoing change. Here international collaboration would attract the best brains from around the world in education, research and development to work on pilot projects that could lead to innovative design solutions in construction as part of planning a low-carbon future based on shared knowledge and experience relevant to each location. These centres would act as regional knowledge banks to inform and direct the work of developers and government towards more progressive and sustainable solutions.

We all need to identify and treasure what is distinctive on our own doorstep first and foremost, no matter how modest it appears. We must value the experiences of our communities, as often we can be blind to them as we compete with the city next door.

We need to 'slow down' to make time for critical thinking so that city leaders can question and appraise their own direction. We all want cities that are safe, inclusive, resilient, sustainable and that take account of good governance, finance and planning, because when we plan the future city, we are committing others to the consequences of the design decisions we are taking now.

▶ **Right:** *Can you guess where they are?*

▶ **Right (middle):** *Four-year-old traditional Chinese street in Chongqing, which has the largest elevated (monorail) mass-transit systems in the world*

▶ **Right (bottom):** *Angela Brady speaking at a sustainable architecture seminar at Ho Chi Minh City school of architecture, Vietnam (MOU with RIBA)*

Second Nature Urban Agriculture: Designing the Productive City

by Andre Viljoen and Professor Katrin Bohn

Andre Viljoen
Architect
Bohn&Viljeon Architects
University of Brighton
www.bohnandviljoen.co.uk

In the future successful cities will be productive in many ways – socially, economically and ecologically. Networks of open space will be essential if cities are to remain desirable and environmentally sustainable. Landscape, like buildings, will become multifunctional, thereby enabling beneficial exchanges between the constructed and natural environments.

The phenomenal pressures on cities are well known; the 2011 UN department of economic and social affairs projection for urbanisation estimates that by 2030 the average world percentage of residents living in urban areas will be 59.9 per cent with 82 per cent in 'more developed regions'. Pressure from urbanisation makes access to open urban spaces an urgent concern.

Furthermore, urban populations are experiencing an unprecedented increase in diet-related ill health. If cities are to thrive, urban planners need to rethink the way cities overcome these challenges to become desirable and environmentally stable.

The concept of Continuous Productive Urban Landscapes (CPULs), developed in 2004 by Bohn&Viljoen, aims to address these problems by proposing an ambitious but achievable strategy for integrating networks of connected open urban spaces that are designed to include food-producing urban agriculture.

Urban agriculture, which refers to the production of fruit, vegetables, fish and sometimes small animals within cities, is not new, and each city and culture will have its own tradition to draw upon. But what is new is the understanding of the multiple benefits, in addition to the production of sustainable food, that CPULs can bring to cities. It is likely that in the future networks of open space will be as important as clusters of buildings.

There is much evidence for these assertions. For example, in 2010 the UN University Institute for Advanced Studies (UNUIAS) issued a policy report on cities and biodiversity and noted that, 'as the rule of interdependent adjacencies in urban ecology has it: the more diversity, and the more collaboration "between unlikely partners", the better the chances for biodiversity, sustainability,

Professor Katrin Bohn
Architect
Bohn&Viljoen Architects
University of Brighton
Technical University of Berlin

▶ *Right: The CPUL concept. Green corridors provide a continuous network of productive open spaces containing routes for pedestrians and cyclists. A variety of fields for urban agriculture and other outdoor work/lesiure activities are located within the network to serve adjacent built-up areas*

and resilience.' The concept of CPULs represents a powerful urban-design instrument for achieving local sustainability while reducing the ecological footprints of cities.

We may conclude that biodiversity delivers or supports much-needed ecosystems and that it can be achieved by creating more, bigger, better and joined resilient and coherent ecological networks... CPULs.

Implementing the CPUL City Concept
There is already a lot of experience in establishing successful urban agriculture projects. Using this knowledge and relating it to the concept of multi-stakeholder planning, a four-point plan of CPUL City Actions has been developed, intended to provide a clear overview of the various processes and activities required to implement CPULs over the long term.

These four actions are: Action U+D = Co-ordinated and mutually supportive Bottom Up + Top Down initiatives and activities; Action VIS = Visualising the Consequences of CPUL proposals; Action IUC = Completing Inventories of existing Urban Capacities for supporting new initiatives; Action R = Researching for Change. It would be rare to find successful long-term projects with not at least three actions evident, even if often they have not been articulated as such.

The UK's Arts and Humanities Research Council (AHRC) is currently funding a research

network to explore how policy pathways can be developed to support the large number of emerging productive landscapes (see http://arts. brighton.ac.uk/projects/utppp/). Setting out clear processes, such as the four CPUL City Actions, should assist stakeholders to realise better and more resilient projects in the future, while discouraging projects that are fundamentally flawed.

If successfully implemented, CPULs have the potential to create more experience for less consumption.

For further information see:
Second Nature Urban Agriculture: Designing Productive Cities, edited by A. Viljoen and K. Bohn, Routledge, 2014
Continuous Productive Urban Landscapes: Designing Urban Agriculture for Sustainable Cities, edited by A. Viljoen, The Architectural Press, 2005

▲ *Above: The CPUL concept is being applied internationally. Spiel/Feld Marzahn, Berlin, Germany was initiated in 2011 as a larger-scale community food-growing project comissioned by the local authority. It was designed by Prof. Katrin Bohn with students from the Technical University of Berlin, who worked with local residents. This project demonstrates how CPUL spaces can reactivate underused public space and result in 'place making'. It has been recognised in Germany for its contribution to the UNESCO decade of education for sustainable development*

▼ *Below: Urban Agriculture Curtain, a prototype by Bohn&Viljeon from 2009, shows how the CPUL concept can be applied within buildings. A vertical hydroponic system was developed with Hadlow College for use in London's Building Centre, to supply salad crops during the 'London Yields' exhibition*

Urban Vegetation and Urban Air Quality

by Professor A. R. MacKenzie

Professor A. R. MacKenzie
Director, Birmingham Institute
of Forest Research (BIFoR)
www.birmingham.ac.uk/bifor

Researchers at the University of Birmingham are investigating the effects of urban vegetation on air quality. In addition to providing a cooling function and other benefits such as improved drainage, vegetation can, in the right places, help to reduce air pollution.

Street canyons — that is, streets enclosed on both sides by high buildings — offer the ideal situation for vegetation to collect pollution. This is because the deposition of pollution to the leaves is accelerated when the pollution is found in high concentrations.

Very large leaf-areas are required for a significant effect; a recent study suggested that covering 60 per cent of the available wall space in a street canyon could produce a 10 per cent reduction in nitrogen-dioxide concentrations. Such large coverage can be difficult to achieve in practice, but 'green walls' are now becoming a more common sight in cities.

When situating vegetation (sometimes referred to in this context as 'green infrastructure'), it is crucial to avoid enclosing heavily trafficked streets with a tree canopy; in such circumstances the ground-level pollution concentrations will increase significantly rather than decrease. Conversely, trees deployed in pedestrianised

▼ **Below:** Newly installed green wall in a street canyon on the Rubens at the Palace hotel in the Victoria Business Improvement District, London

areas (for instance, in precincts and courtyards) are always beneficial in reducing air pollution and could make the air in those areas cleaner than in neighbouring streets with traffic and possibly even cleaner than in the surrounding countryside.

Because the urban context is so important in determining the effects the vegetation has on the environment, it is crucial to maintain a close connection between a piece of green infrastructure and the benefits that infrastructure is intended to bring. It is then important to consider whether the infrastructure will be resilient in the face of the rapid change we expect to see in cities over the next few decades.

▲ **Above:** *Laycock Street, Islington, London*

▶ **Right:** *Oxford Market*

The 'Urban Futures Method', designed by UK scientists led by the University of Birmingham, provides a way of improving the resilience of any kind of intervention, not least changes designed to 'green' a city, and can greatly increase

returns on investment in urban infrastructure.

The Urban Futures Method is built into the Trees and Design Action Group's *Trees in the Townscape: A Guide for Decision Makers*.

The Cooling Effects of Trees

by Professor Roland Ennos

Professor Roland Ennos
Professor of Biological Sciences,
University of Hull
www.hull.ac.uk

Researchers at the University of Manchester, led by myself, are investigating the cooling effect of trees and grass. Trees and grass improve the thermal environment of the city in two ways.

First, trees cool cities by altering their energy balance. They do this partly by reflecting more of the incoming sunlight, but more importantly by allowing water to evaporate from their leaves. We have shown that healthy, fast-growing trees can remove up to 40 per cent of the incoming energy, but that trees in a poor condition are much less effective.

Second, shade from trees cools people by shielding them from the sun's radiation, reducing how hot they feel by up to 7°C in hot sunny weather, and greatly increasing their comfort. Trees and grass also reduce surface temperatures by up to 20°C, as the infra-red picture below shows, though they do require an adequate supply of water.

Our current research is investigating how we can maximise the cooling benefits of trees and grass by choosing the right species and optimising their conditions for growth.

▼ *Below (top): In the shade of the trees – urban coolth, Chicago*

▼ *Below (bottom): Energy exchanges during a summer's day in a city park (left) and downtown area (right)*

▼ *Below: Infra-red thermal picture of a park. People cluster in the shade of the trees (blue) as this is cooler than grass (yellow) and much cooler than tarmac (red)*

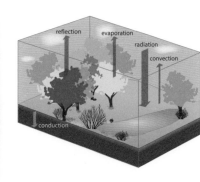

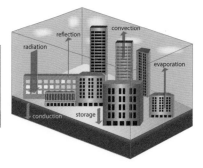

The Trees and Design Action Group

by Sue James

Sue James
Architect
Trees and Design Action Group
www.tdag.org.uk

The Trees and Design Action Group (TDAG) is considered unique in that it has brought together a wide range of participants in urban development who share a common vision to protect and promote urban trees for the many benefits they bring to both people and the built and natural environment.

These benefits are now quantifiable thanks to the development of i-tree eco by the USDA Forest Service. In New York City, for example, it has been shown that an investment of $1 per tree can return $5 in quantifiable benefits.

This ability to undertake cost-benefit analysis on urban trees helps development teams and city officials alike and provides baseline information on which to make effective decisions regarding the urban forest.

TDAG has shown that much can be achieved when government departments, local authorities, utility companies, built-environment professionals, developers, planners, tree specialists and academics work together to promote understanding and recognition of the key role the urban forest plays in the present and future resilience of our cities.

▼ **Below:** *From 'Trees in the Townscape: A Guide for Decision Makers', available at www.tdag.org.uk*

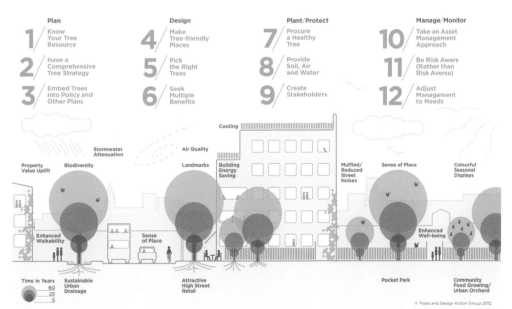

Adapting Buildings and Cities for Climate Change

by Professor Susan Roaf

Professor Susan Roaf
School of the Built Environment
Professor of Architectural Engineering
Heriot-Watt University, Edinburgh
www.sbe.hw.ac.uk

We live in a rapidly changing world with extremes of weather, a warming climate, soaring costs of food and energy and a shaky global economy. These changes are forcing us to rethink the way we design buildings and cities to make them climate-ready, more resilient and safer for future generations.

Never in the history of the architectural, engineering or planning professions has there been a time when so much change is required to produce *fit-for-purpose* solutions. Even today we see around us designs that are causing problems, not offering answers.

The passing era of cheap energy, when good buildings were understood largely as exotic sculptures given names like 'infinity', 'gherkin' or 'toast rack' to distinguish their fashionable excellence, must inevitably be replaced by an age when design will be measured by how well a

▼ **Below:** *Image of Urban Heat Island (UHI), Atlanta, Georgia, showing temperature distribution, with blue indicating cool temperatures, red warm and hot areas shown as white. The night-time effect of UHIs is devastating during heat waves because the city stays hot all night, unlike rural areas that cool down. European cities with parks and lower, less shiny buildings have lower UHI impacts than tall, shiny US cities*

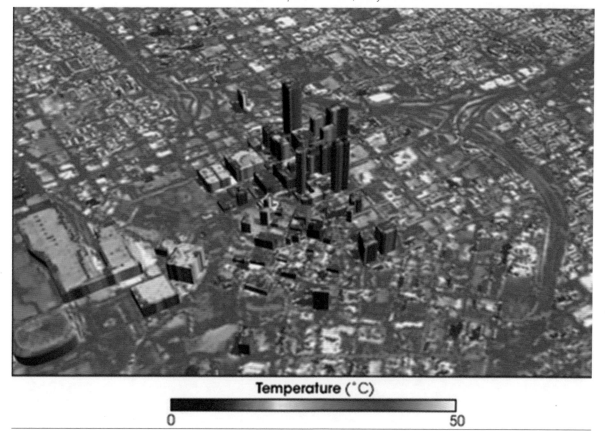

Temperature (˚C)

0   50

building behaves in extremes of heat, cold, flooding, drought and storm winds. The durability of a company brand will be measured by how low its fossil-fuel energy costs are, as an indication of its lack of vulnerability to soaring grid-energy prices.

The business continuity planning profession has already singled out for concern building types that are likely to fail catastrophically if electricity blackouts occur, as is increasingly happening around the world. In the 21st century we will have to build more *resilience* into our buildings, businesses and lifestyles. Resilience is a measure of the capacity of a system to adapt to changing conditions and to maintain or regain functionality and vitality in the face of stress or disturbance (www.resilientdesign.org).

In 2009 we published the second edition of our book *Adapting Buildings and Cities for Climate Change*, which became required reading for thinkers in the field. It tells you about how hot, wet, cold, dry and windy it will become and discusses many design challenges and solutions (www.sciencedirect.com/science/book/9781856177207).

Common sense in the way we design is now vital. We must follow our instincts on what will indeed produce *safer* buildings for the future.

Simulation models do not deal at all, or well, with such issues. Simple sensible solutions start with Resilient City Planning:

» Do not build on floodplains.
» Require good solar orientation so buildings can run optimally on free solar energy.
» Mandate narrow floor plans so rooms can be naturally ventilated (required today in Berlin).
» Design green places throughout the city to reduce the heat island effect.
» Allow the city to breathe, with natural ventilation paths for *good* prevailing winds kept open.
» Reduce the height of buildings to reduce the energy used to build and run them and the 'peakyness' of electricity demand, which causes the power failures.

▼ **Below:** *Two neighbouring buildings on the Corniche at Nice in the south of France. The contrast highlights the madness of modern architecture that shuts out one of the most pleasant climates in Europe at a huge cost in terms of energy and greenhouse-gas emissions as well as durability and the thermal comfort and delight so patently available in the traditional building*

At the building level:
» Understand the local micro-climate and design to use free energy from it where possible, with the use of planting or earth energy to pre-condition air supplies.
» Avoid overheating and over-glazing, especially on western façades and roofs.
» Design all buildings to be able to operate in natural ventilation mode for some or most of the year as well as during power failures.
» Control air-infiltration pathways.
» Storm-proof the building by controlling winds around it and providing wind sheltering.
» Waterproof the building with good water run-off, collection and landscaping.
» Use the building form to match required indoor climates with different locations inside.
» Use thermal mass and energy storage to load-shift and load-shave peak energy demands.
» Provide multiple options to adapt indoor micro-climates to requirements including shutters, blinds, shades, curtains, multiple options for opening windows, and balconies.
» Use high levels of insulation to keep heat inside in winter and outside in summer.

The above list does not represent rocket science, and yet is often overlooked by too many designers.

Adaptation is not a product but is about a mindset and a process. The first step is to recognise the urgent need to build resilience into our lives and the next is to educate ourselves in what will work, and what will not, in a very different future.

There are many organisations working in this field now (see for instance: www.weadapt.org; www.ukcip.org.uk and www.climatexchange.org.uk.)

The best designers will increasingly look to create buildings that will still work well in 2030 or 2050, because the best clients will increasingly demand them.

Not all professions, or professionals, will survive. We have known for over a decade that the conventional model of building design for the last century of cheap energy is not fit-for-purpose in the 21st century (www.cibse.org/pdfs/terrywyattaddress.pdf). The real question now is: in a rapidly changing world, who will be the fittest to survive?

Perhaps Steve Jobs had the answer when he said that the important thing with a business model was to 'Get It'. We all need to 'get' *resilience*.

◄ *Left: In cities around the world modern buildings are falling empty and being demolished, often long before their historic neighbours. Many are simply less well-designed for the local climates and consequently suffer from over-heating, very high energy bills and occupant dissatisfaction.*
As we experience more extreme weather events, city authorities must prioritise the need to promote climate ready and resilient buildings and discourage buildings with poor climatic design as they responsibly manage the evolution of their urban landscapes. This image shows a number of more modern buildings being demolished around St Andrew's Square during the Edinburgh Festival while the robust and attractive, traditional stone building next door is retained.
For more information on Scotland's leading-edge activities in the field of policy development for climate adaptation and mitigation across its built environments and landscapes see:
www.climatexchange.org.uk

Education, Research and Development
by Professor Alan Penn

Professor Alan Penn
Dean, The Bartlett Faculty of the Built
Environment UCL
www.bartlett.ucl.ac.uk

As China urbanises ever more rapidly it has become apparent that there is a severe shortage of the high-level design and planning talent required to deliver the future to which the People's Republic aspires.

While the Chinese system for project finance and delivery continues to astound the rest of the world, many western observers have a feeling of *déjà vu* when they look at projects on the ground. Functional zoning in a car-dependent city grid is the norm, with gated communities and dispersed suburbs for the new affluent classes and dense high-rise living for the less well off. Heritage is under threat or treated as a museum piece and landscape manicured for leisure visitors. The ubiquitous multi-level shopping mall has become the focus for urban life, just as the high-rise office building and industrial park have become the focus for work and production.

This feeling of *déjà vu* stems from western experience during the industrial revolution. This is mirrored by China today, albeit on a highly compressed timescale. It is for this reason that the west has something specific to offer China at the moment. We have made mistakes in the past, and the UK's education and research base in our

▼ **Below:** *Old meets new in Chongqing*

universities and technology organisations has found out how to foster creativity and innovation by learning from these mistakes, and above all has 'learned how to learn'.

There is no such thing as a fixed answer to any challenge. Instead we must educate our professionals continually to move their goals, to work analytically and to take no shortcuts. It is here that China has the most to gain from working with the west. If we can help to create a culture of continuous innovation in the Chinese planning system there is hope that the greatest building project the world has yet seen can avoid repeating the errors of the past and achieve a sustainable future.

Over the last few years a number of leading UK universities have been investing heavily in relations with China. New campuses have been built by some, memorandums of understanding signed with others, and visiting delegations have travelled in each direction. Recently, the Bartlett Faculty of the Built Environment at UCL hosted a training programme for 31 senior planning professionals from Guandong province. During the two-week period they received lectures from some of the UK's leading authorities on planning and sustainability, visited a range of sites and were able to question their professional counterparts. Feedback suggests that at least in Guandong, some of the UK's experience will help China to develop in a more sustainable

way. Other provinces are now following this lead by sending senior staff to the UK.

The Bartlett is already the main UK destination for undergraduate and postgraduate students from China. They come to study architecture, planning and urban design through a wide range of programmes from BSc and Masters to PhD. The core skills they gain are creative innovation coupled to science and critical analysis. They learn to bring together arts, science and technology in pursuit of sustainable forms of architecture and urban development.

Europe, the UK and London are uniquely suited to helping China. While the US urbanised very rapidly during the 20th century, it did so on virgin green land as a newly developing nation. The challenges faced by Europe, by contrast, were those of a mature civilisation that needed to adapt rapidly to the future. This is much closer to the Chinese situation today.

The UK, and London in particular, host the world's largest and richest cluster of advanced built-environment firms, ranging from creative architectural practices to advanced multi-disciplinary engineers and the real-estate, surveying, legal and financial services firms that provide the supply chain for global urbanisation. In order to operate globally, all the main US architecture practices have London offices. This is where the global supply chain for built environment services is

based and where there is the best supply of graduate talent. The UK has a uniquely global understanding of the different social and institutional contexts of regions around the world, the way different regional construction-sector firms are organised and the economic and regulatory regimes at play.

The UK's 'ecosystem' of built-environment sector businesses is supported by the world's most advanced cluster of built-environment research institutions in its universities. It was in Cambridge, Sheffield and UCL that the main innovations in advanced built-environment computing originated in the 1980s and 1990s, and where the main advances in transformational technologies of mobile, ubiquitous and peer-to-peer networks and crowd-sourced data are currently under development. It is here that these advances are now being transferred to application through Building Information Models (BIM), following the UK government's far-sighted policy to require their use in all government construction projects. New impetus has been given to the rapid and agile development of advanced fabrication and off-site manufacture, and to the exploitation of advanced manufacturing processes for genuinely creative architecture.

Given the challenges that China faces today, and her aspirations for a prosperous and harmonious future, learning from the UK offers a short cut to success.

Evaluating the Energy Performance of Your Property

by Dr Judit Kimpian

Dr Judit Kimpian, Architect
Carbonbuzz
Director of Sustainable Architecture
and Research at AHR
www.ahr-global.com

There is growing evidence that current legislation is not achieving the expected reductions in the actual energy use of buildings – and, if anything, can have significant unintended consequences. Portfolio holders in particular are taking note of the associated commercial risks when new 'low-carbon' buildings and refurbishments fall short of performance expectations.

CarbonBuzz is an RIBA|CIBSE crowdsourcing platform for the design community and property industry that aims to help understand why the gap between predicted and operational energy use exists and to close this gap by publishing evidence, advice and case studies.

We use cloud-computing technology to offer built-environment professionals a simple and quick way to upload, share and benchmark building energy-use data. The majority of the 800 or so members manage their data and benchmark anonymously, but users can also showcase their expertise by publishing projects and results.

A key feature of the website is that energy consumption is displayed as an easy-to-read 'energy bar' that shows annual consumption in either

$kWh/(m^2\ yr)$ or kg $CO_2/(m^2\ yr)$ equivalents. The bar can display either fuel consumption or, where the data is available, energy use apportioned to heating, cooling, auxiliary power, lighting and small power loads.

A user-friendly interface allows building owners to track the energy consumption of their portfolios as well as improvements in performance over time – for instance, British Land has recently achieved a 39 per cent reduction in the energy consumption of its portfolio.

The type of energy literacy advocated by CarbonBuzz makes the Soft Landings process more robust and accountable. Using CarbonBuzz, architects, engineers and end users can for the first time log how energy-consumption targets are met at key stages and demonstrate that investment in low-energy measures has brought about the expected returns. What a revelation that will be…

CarbonBuzz is beginning to provide industry feedback about the scale of the performance gap. Analysis of the data demonstrates that on average most buildings consume between 1.5 and 2.5 times the energy of the declared design-stage calculations and that in the case of offices and buildings for education this anomaly arises largely from increased use of electrical energy.

At the root of the performance gap is the fact that to comply with building regulations designers need only to assess a building's energy consumption potential using calculations based on idealised operating circumstances. Yet recent CarbonBuzz surveys show that built-environment professionals and policy-makers assume that compliance is a reliable way of improving operational energy use.

New procurement models targeting operational energy use are emerging, which will reward those with a track record in achieving better value for their clients. With post-occupancy evaluations

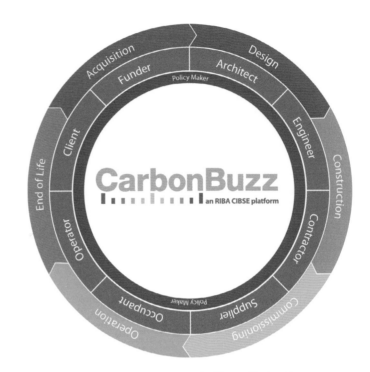

soon to be incorporated into the procurement of all public projects, the productivity benefits of lower energy and maintenance costs will become more pronounced.

For now, however, CarbonBuzz has achieved what few thought

possible. Knowing what your building consumes has become the 'new cool'.

▲ *Above: CarbonBuzz – energy tracking over the building life-cycle*

▼ *Below: Loxford School published with annual energy-consumption data on the CarbonBuzz platform*

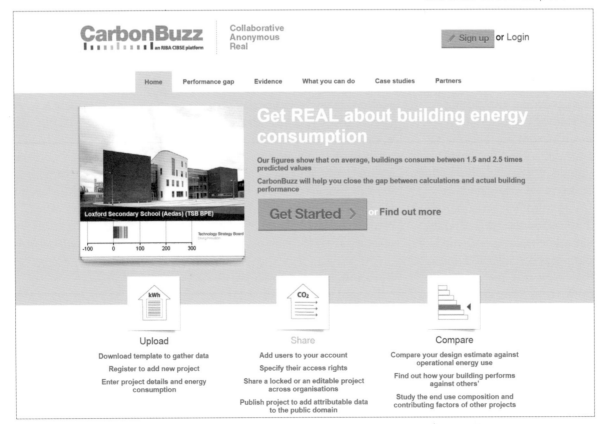

Creating Sustainable Communities: Process, Place, People

by Charles Campion

Charles Campion, Architect
Partner, John Thompson & Partners
www.jtp.co.uk

One of the most urgent challenges facing humankind is how to build more sustainable cities, towns, villages and neighbourhoods. These are places that consume fewer resources, create less pollution and have the capacity to adapt to changing circumstances over time, with the resources in place to meet people's everyday needs.

Over the past 20 years, working across a wide range of projects, JTP has found that sustainable development is most effectively achieved if the knowledge and commitment of the community and stakeholders are engaged at every stage of the design and planning process – techniques John Thompson first used when commissioned to refurbish Lea View House, London, a run-down council block that was suffering from high rates of crime and anti-social behaviour.

Along the way, we have learned that it is crucial to recognise the difference between participation and consultation. Participation means inviting people to get involved in shaping their own future. Consultation without participation is simply asking people to agree what has already been decided by others and can prompt a negative reaction.

We have therefore pioneered structured 'charrette' processes which enable stakeholders to work together with professionals in a creative way that ultimately adds value at all levels – physical, social, environmental and economic – and leads to better, more sustainable and more valuable places.

A 'charrette' is an interactive, multi-day design workshop in which stakeholders (often including the community) work directly with a multi-disciplinary design team to generate a specific vision and masterplan. Charrette working provides benefits in terms of input and quality, and can greatly increase the speed of the design and approval process. It is a hands-on approach where ideas are translated into plans and drawings and participants are taken through feedback loops to build understanding and support. Feedback loops occur when a design is proposed, reviewed, changed and re-presented for further review.

The three key attributes of the charrette team are: the ability to engage and inspire stakeholders; the ability to successfully manage the logistics, mechanics and teamwork of a charrette process; and the skills of visioning, masterplanning and effective graphic communication.

One of the best recent examples of local stakeholder involvement took place in Scarborough, England. At the turn of this century the town was on the brink of terminal decline when Yorkshire Forward, the former Regional Development Agency (RDA), set up a process to engage the town to rethink itself and its future. The outcome was a Visionary Renaissance Charter for the town and the establishment of a Renaissance Town Team with power to sign off investment from the RDA.

In the last decade Scarborough has transformed into what has been described as a 'thriving enterprise hotspot'. An initial public-sector strategic investment of over £20 million stimulated a private-sector response over ten times greater. In 2010 Scarborough won the award of Europe's Most Enterprising Town from the EC and in 2014, as a result of a process driven by the Town Team, it was awarded University Technical College status by the government. It was the coming together of stakeholders to create a consensus vision that gave the town a clear and supported roadmap to the future.

We have also demonstrated that the charrette approach can be worthwhile for the private sector. The breakthrough came at Caterham, where a five-day participatory charrette considered what a large-scale developer should do to transform redundant army barracks. The process transformed the community's previous hostility to new development into positive support for the creation of a mixed-use neighbourhood that increased the development value of the site by £50 million, with over £2.5 million of new community facilities, owned and run by a not-for-profit Community Development Trust. In addition, because the community was fully involved, the planning application moved quickly through the approval system.

As JTP continues to strive to create sustainable communities across the UK and around the world, it is encouraging to see government commitment to stakeholder involvement in planning has increased dramatically. The Scottish government is promoting charrette processes as a cornerstone of good planning for both the public and private sectors and in the US charrettes are deployed as a first response to natural disasters, bringing together communities to plan for recovery.

Participatory planning at all scales of development focuses on the real needs of communities, adding value by improving quality, building consensus, and speeding up delivery. Charrette methodologies can play a vital role in taking the sustainable-urbanism agenda forward by helping to build the places and communities that will promote healthy and happy lives for our children and grandchildren around the globe.

▼ **Below:** *Design output from a JTP multi-day charrette at Changzhi Island for developers Greentown*

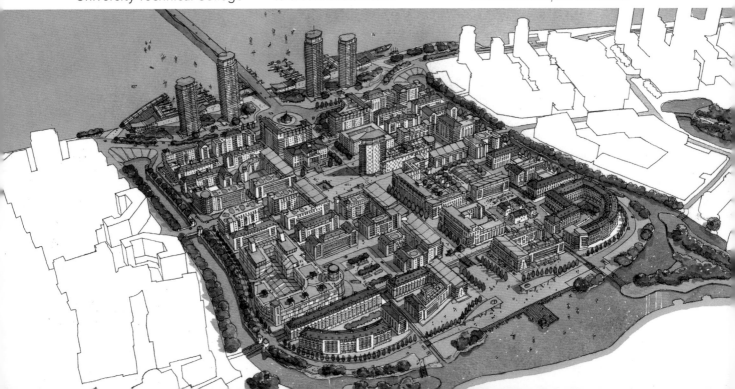

Protecting the Uniqueness of Each City
by David Twohig and Robert Tincknell

David Twohig
Head of Design and Placemaking,
Battersea Power Station Development
Company
Author of *Living in Wonderland* (2014)

Robert Tincknell
Chief Executive Officer, Battersea
Power Station Development Company
www.batterseapowerstation.co.uk

The World Health Organisation forecasts that the population of the world's cities is set to increase by 3 billion by 2050. This is set against the backdrop of globalisation, where the individuality of our cities is being replaced by homogenous and characterless shopping centres and apartment towers all filled with the same stuff.

Over the next 15 years China is set to urbanise 300 million people and to build an urban area equivalent in size to North America. In the greatest period of urbanisation in human history, the buildings and places we are designing and developing leave a lot to be desired. The world's cities increasingly conform to a one-stop solution and those people who are relocating to them are subject to identikit lives.

The biggest challenge facing China is the rapid scale of development. In 2000 Shanghai had a population of 16 million people, which had risen to 23 million by the time of the 2010 census. That is nearly 700,000 additional people to be accommodated every year.

It would be a challenge for any urban planning authority to manage such relentless growth, but when you apply it across a nation of 1.3 billion people and 100 metropolitan areas that have a population of more than 1 million, the scale of the task begins to become apparent. How could any nation manage such rapid growth without wanting to find a one-stop solution?

Unfortunately, that is what is happening across China, where each city is a copy and paste of its neighbour. South-facing residential towers line up like modern-day Terracotta Warriors above shiny shopping centres. Millions of people are migrating from rural farmland to be subjected to high-density city grids dominated by vast future-proofed road networks.

There is little recognition that it is urban areas with a unique identity and authenticity which will succeed in attracting outside investment and encouraging talent to relocate – both of which are crucial to a region's economic success. China has only to study the cities of Hangzhou and Qingdao to see how a rich natural and built environment can be a catalyst for prosperity.

Too many urban areas are turning to artificial mechanisms such as tax incentivisation to attract businesses, ignoring the creation of quality places. The current strategy may appear to work during the initial stages of manufacturing development, when low-skilled workers move from rural areas without employment prospects to seek low-skilled jobs elsewhere. However, these unconsidered urban environments are not sustainable over the coming decades as the population's education and prospects improve.

One of the problems is that the central management of so many metropolitan areas is counterproductive. Competition between urban centres should be encouraged and local planning authorities should be enabled to manage their own built environments. This will encourage cities to capitialise on their unique and specific attributes rather than choose the path of universal development, which renders them no different to their neighbours and means they lack a competitive edge.

China has a rich and diverse history. It needs to use that history to enable development rather than bulldoze its past in order to create homogenous platforms for regeneration. It is a nation with financial capability and resources, but these need to be handled in a way that generates new neighbourhoods with human scale and a unique identity, where traditional hutongs are protected to create city centres that are walkable and mountains are retained to create urban environments with an identity to rival San Francisco or Cape Town.

Taikang Road and Xintiandi in Shanghai are good sxamples where quasi-historic centres with a human scale have gone a long way towards humanising areas surrounded by residential tower buildings.

The wave of people relocating to China's cities is so great that it is understandable that

planning authorities reach for a default single solution. But they would be better served to spend time further researching long-term sustainable models for building great cities.

Collaboration with the best talent from around the world should be encouraged in order to learn from the successes and failures of previous models. Care needs to be taken if quality of life is to mirror economic development for future generations living in China.

▼ *Below: Shanghai's identikit apartment towers lined up like rows of Terracotta Warriors*

New City: Old City
A Design Process Locked into Context, Community and Climate

by Roddy Langmuir

In 2009 we were asked to form a team to design a 'new' carbon-neutral town for 60,000 people in Libya's Green Mountain region. I've often worried about the baggage we carry with us when we design in a completely new environment. How can we possibly contribute the right kind of livable buildings, placemaking and public realm in a context that at the outset is entirely unfamiliar to us?

Architecture has been shown to travel badly and most of us have no interest in adding to the appalling global trade in buildings as style products. If good design is not to be just about style and surface it must surely be about process – the process we go through as designers in testing our brief, analysing context, understanding specific cultural needs and addressing micro-to-global climate issues.

Roddy Langmuir
Architect
Practice Leader, Cullinan Studio
www.cullinanstudio.com

▼ *Below: A ribbon of connected neighbourhoods in a productive landscape*

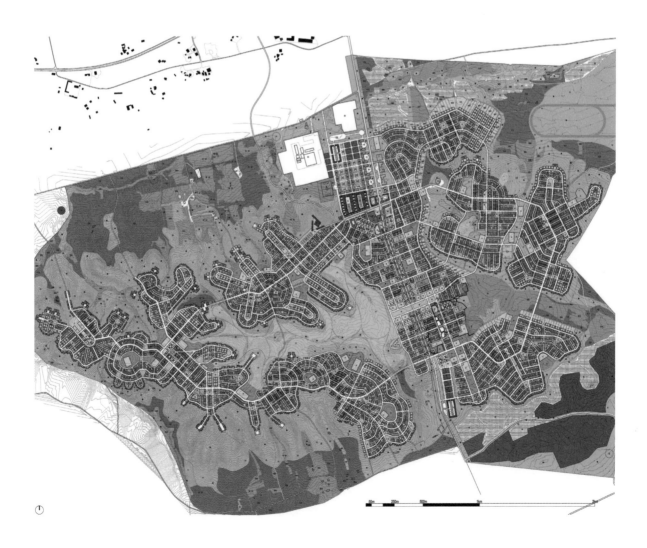

I wouldn't claim this design process is a preserve of UK architects – just that we in the UK have wonderful examples to draw on and that the complex interwoven social and physical history of our island has forced us to respond with architectural storytelling rooted in the particular qualities of each place.

In terms of cultural diversity, the UK is a complex matrix of different cultures and ethnicities, often integrated in mixed communities that share the facilities and services of a neighbourhood. The historic context often defines our sense of place in the UK.

Our land has been worked and reworked for millennia, creating multi-layered natural and built environments that juxtapose old with new to challenge us as designers to connect with context. Our seasonal climate challenges us to respond to scenarios of cooling and heating and our interdisciplinary, collaborative approach to design can help us meet our responsibility to address global climate change.

At Cullinan Studio we have always used these three principles – responding to context, community and climate – to define our architectural approach. The architecture then has something more weighty to draw on to support the aesthetic judgements that must be made throughout an evolving design.

As we balance the parts, compose façades and forms, manipulate daylight and enjoy the textural contrasts of materials, each small decision is made much more powerful because it is underpinned by the strength and longevity of more vital and expansive themes.

Shahat Garden City
Context: topography and land use
So we began our work on Shahat Garden City with many, many questions and a great deal of listening. We mapped everything of value on our site – ecology, archaeology, businesses, productive farmland and so on – until we were left with the land that had least value.

This was where we would build 14 new walkable neighbourhoods, contouring the rocky hilltops. We had researched the expansion and densification of the existing town of Shahat close to the World Heritage Site of Cyrene, but the solution to create a large new town on greenfield and brownfield land was driven by UNESCO's archaeological buffer zone around Cyrene, the most intact and dramatically sited example of an ancient Greek city anywhere.

Community: privacy and proximity
We developed an entirely new set of plot sizes and guidelines to create housing that would deliver the right balance of privacy and community in

self-shaded streets to a density that enabled the neighbourhood centres to be easily reached.

Climate: productive landscapes

A network of paths and a hierarchy of forests create shade and shelter. Agriculture is scaled from the extended plot garden to smallholdings and the wadi farms that surround each neighbourhood. A botanic garden lies at the heart of the 'Garden City' to preserve a biodiversity recognised as internationally important. Landscape provides an integrated ecosystem that recognises that public landscape would only survive if it is productive.

Solar farms, wind farms, energy from waste, integrated tourism and inward investment from local construction were some of the initiatives which used the project as part of its sustainable realisation.

Singapore Management University

More often as architects we are working in a far more complex urban context. An example of this kind of urban integration is the Singapore Management University (SMU). In 2004 we won an international competition to design a new downtown campus for SMU. Our 240,000-square-metre masterplan was built from scratch in the heart of Singapore's developed cityscape. With a necklace of open courts, the plan encourages three connecting strands to flow through the site: the landscape, the surrounding business community, and the cooling breezes of the micro-climatic response.

Context: landscape

A sense of open space and visual connection is maintained between the historic landmarks of the cathedral, National Museum and the Singapore Art Museum. There are three connecting tiers of landscape – roof-level gardens, ground-level parkland and basement courts.

Communities: students, public, business

A mixed-use concourse of retail, business start-ups and shared teaching and learning space merges the city's public and business communities with students of business. The university is stratified vertically, with more private teaching space at the higher levels so departments can be interchanged between buildings.

Climate: learning from history

Street trees, overhangs and narrow high-planted courts modify the heat and humidity to reduce the amount of space that needs to be air conditioned artificially. We learned from the old streets and buildings of Singapore to create shaded transitional spaces with breezeways that harness pressure differences across buildings.

These have now been adopted as favourite workspaces by the students.

To be sustainable, buildings have to find their place in the continuity of history as yet another layer or weave to enrich the urban tapestry rather than fight against it. All the low-energy gizmos – the bells and whistles of green wash – are little more than a distraction from a building's longevity, from its integration and adoption by its community, and from the way it should build on its neighbours' strengths to leave a better whole.

▼ **Below:** Balancing privacy with community.

The Living City: the Role of Technology in Planning, Design and Constructing More Sustainable Cities

by Andrew Comer

Andrew Comer
Civil Engineer
Partner and Director, Cities,
BuroHappold Engineering
www.burohappold.com

What are the underlying drivers for our future cities and towns, how will they need to perform, why focus on them, and what is wrong with current best practice? These questions are wide-ranging and the serious challenges associated with this subject must be addressed urgently.

The key drivers globally include population growth, demographic shifts and the unrelenting depletion of our natural resources. These phenomena contribute to climate change and increasingly volatile weather extremes and natural disasters. In addition, second-order 'drivers' are at work: reduced public-sector spending, requiring more to be delivered for less and the need to engage private equity; the globalisation of trade, which means cities now compete with each other; major corporations facing consumer pressure to take their environmental and social responsibilities more seriously.

Despite the fact that half the world's people live in an urban environment, cities are not very efficient: they contribute a major proportion of the world's carbon footprint and this will increase as their populations expand. Yet the larger 'platform' the city offers should mean greater efficiencies are achievable per unit of effort. In planning terms, there is a need for an improved approach to developing co-ordinated and evidence-based policies for the environmental, social and economic aspects of a development. Cities must have a sustainable economic base, or they will have no future. Even with clear business cases, raising capital investment for projects is challenging. For development to progress in a sustainable manner, clear ground rules and performance-based targets should be established at public levels, and mechanisms found to engage private-sector capital and provide capital funding for investment in return for revenue streams – similar to the way the railway, roads and canals were created to help spread the Industrial Revolution.

There is an emerging recognition of technology's role in helping to improve the efficiencies of cities and the quality of life of their citizens. The important point is that we need to create or recreate cities as sustainably as possible, to make them ultimately 'livable', and the appropriate application of science and technology will help to achieve this. This is not a revolutionary approach – ever since the

▶ *Overleaf:* Tun Razak Exchange, Kuala Lumpur. Client: 1MDB

Industrial Revolution the application of advances in science and technology has driven advances in social, environmental and economic terms. The vision of 'smart', 'green', 'healthy' and sustainable cities is well documented. But the real debate should be how this vision is converted into reality. This is one of Buro Happold's key focuses: to help move from rhetoric to action and to push the boundaries of the planning, design and construction of cities to create what we term 'The Living City' (burohappold.com/thelivingcity).

Good design requires people who can respond to the challenge of developing the 'Future City' including professionals who can deliver a responsive, adaptable and sustainable set of infrastructures capable of supporting a society living in energy-efficient, healthy and enjoyable environments where people can live, work and socialise. Smart technologies can assist by ensuring a more effective use of resources and by providing information that supports further improvements and provides evidence of progress. But the fundamentals of design still have to be established: less need to travel, buildings oriented to take advantage of micro-climates, green spaces for amenity and health, optimisation of development around geophysical, environmental and cultural features, and connectivity with existing communities and infrastructures.

Contractors and their supply chains must convert to a low-waste, highly skilled industry championing sustainable construction techniques and value-driven, well constructed products. Reliance on old practices is partly a result of the market's low margins, reducing investment in new techniques, but it is also due to clients placing capital cost considerations ahead of whole-lifecycle costs as well as the fragmented and litigious nature of the various parties to the construction process. There is growing complexity in the roles and functions associated with urban development, but the challenge is clear: professional engineers are now required, as they were over a century ago, to act as the lynchpin connecting applied technology and infrastructure or city planning and design, to broker optimal responses to competing issues and to provide strong leadership.

At the same time, city administrators and developers need to reconsider and improve economic models to leverage greater benefits for a wider society. As practitioners within the field we must use every tool available to achieve the necessary step-change.

The question is not whether we can afford to pursue this avenue but rather can we afford not to? A fundamental shift in our approach to planning, design and construction is required to safeguard our planet and to achieve The Living City.

Low Carbon and Cities: the Future

by Simon Sturgis

Simon Sturgis
Architect
Managing Director,
Sturgis Carbon Profiling llp
www.sturgiscarbonprofiling.com

Searching for a zero-carbon future has focused our thinking on how buildings are made and used, as well as on their disposal. It is said that in nature there is no waste, which suggests total resource efficiency. The current cycle of making, using and disposing of buildings runs entirely counter to this principle. If we are to move to a zero-carbon trajectory for the life of our buildings, then we have to change the way we make them. We will need to think of a building as an evolving process rather than a box that is 'finished' at a point in time.

People are constantly evolving and changing. Individual behaviour has a direct and significant impact on carbon emissions; changes in collective behaviour can bring even greater benefits. These can reduce a significant proportion of a building or city's emissions and can be informed by culture, innovation, and/or the nature of the buildings in which we live and work.

Future low-carbon buildings will be made of components that are 100 per cent recyclable, either directly by reusing them 'as is', or indirectly, as in 'use what you have, to make what you will have'. Waste from consumables will be used

to manufacture building materials as well as to power the fabrication process. Total flexibility will be fundamental: buildings will be capable of being changed, dismantled, moved and reassembled. We have achieved this in London, dismantling and moving a 3,500-square-metre building two kilometres with substantial material, carbon and cost savings.

What sort of industrial processes will be needed to deliver buildings that are capable of continual evolution? Traditional processes are linear, producing materials that are cut and assembled with resulting waste. 3D printing, which is evolving fast, is the closest we get to zero waste since you use only the exact quantity you need to make something, and you make it where it is needed. Add that to ideas of 'self assembly' and renewable materials, and you

▼ *Below: Cycle of reuse for aluminium*

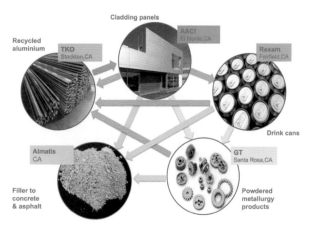

are closing in on a truly zero-carbon building typology.

So who will design these buildings? The basic processes for zero-carbon assembly, enabling 100 per cent reuse, will be highly sophisticated. This points to the likes of advanced product designers using intelligent software that is able to track and manage large amounts of materials data. People will collectively decide what they want of a building and communicate their requirements, ensuring that what is required is what is delivered. Because total flexibility is inherent, change can easily be achieved. Everything I have described above is happening right now, but not necessarily all together. The important reality is that innovation will point the way to delivering inherently

low-carbon buildings that are radically different to most of what we produce today. For high-carbon investments such as public buildings, durability and resilience will become paramount. Today's assumed lifespan of 50 to 60 years will no longer be acceptable.

Our buildings should be made from materials that are seen as 'on loan' from our environment. Recycling existing buildings either whole or in bits is therefore fundamental to a low-carbon future. It has been said that most buildings are already built. Retaining and retrofitting is inherently low carbon in terms of materials because the emissions have already been released. In whole-life carbon terms, even a new Passivhaus cannot match a retrofit.

▲ **Above:** *GIS carbon map of Heathrow Airport*

For a city to have a zero-carbon trajectory means that over time fewer new materials and less energy will be introduced. Waste will be reduced and reused because the city, as a complex organism, will be predominantly feeding on itself. Redundant materials from one building will go to creating another with waste providing the necessary power.

The design of buildings will facilitate this 'carbon exchange'. Components capable of beneficial reuse will have a high tradable value and whole buildings will be sold and moved to new locations. Enhanced efficiency and innovation will mean larger buildings can be made from the same quantity of materials as those they replace.

So we need to think about carbon emissions and their mitigation holistically, looking at people's behaviour, building fabrication and the organism of the city.

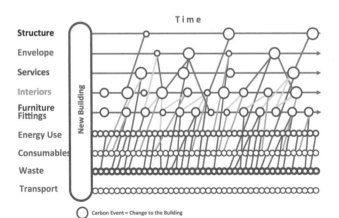

◀ **Left (top):** *Carbon map of a building's evolution: a new café is created from energy and materials from itself*

◀ **Left:** *A building is an organism not a box. The building feeds on itself. A map of all carbon transactions over time.*

How to Survive and Thrive in the 21st century

by Justin Bere

Justin Bere
Architect
Director, Bere Architects
www.bere.co.uk

In Europe our average continuous energy usage for everything from food and clothing to transport and homes is 6,000 watts, 24/7. This level of consumption is only possible thanks to the combustion of precious fuels produced by the decomposition of millions of years of plant life.

Every day across the world we burn the equivalent of all the plants growing on this planet over a year to meet our energy needs. The benefits of this consumption have been enormous for much of mankind, but for the planet it has been disastrous. We now know that it has brought us – and the 10 million other species that live with us here on earth – to the brink of climate catastrophe. Burning fossil fuels for the production of energy must stop.

What can replace fossil fuels and still meet the needs of an advanced society? Here are two options:
» The generation of abundant clean energy.
» The generation of more modest amounts of clean energy.

Since time is running out, it seems most sensible to assume that in the immediate future we are unlikely to have access to abundant clean energy. So to make the most of what we have, we must reduce demand by every means we can.

The Passive approach simply avoids waste while at the same time improving human living conditions. This involves some science, but most important is a lot of care to ensure that every drop of harvested or consumed energy is treasured. Ninety per cent overall energy savings can be quite reliably achieved in retrofit, for between only 3 and 10 per cent additional project cost on top of a standard refurbishment.

Until recently much of the focus was on offsetting energy requirements (CSH Level 6, for example), which means over-generating clean electricity in summer to offset the dirty energy still used in winter.

▼ *Below: The Mildmay Centre, Newington Green, London (certified Passive House)*

But because power-station requirements are based on peak grid demand, 'offsetting' energy does little to reduce the number of power stations we are deemed to need.

With Passive design, however, the 90 per cent energy savings that have been noted in building-performance evaluations can be maintained throughout the winter months. A certified Passive House is so efficient that on overcast winter days most of the total energy demand (including heat, TV, lights, cooker, and so on) of an average domestic house can be supplied by about 30 to 40 square metres of photovoltaics. The further energy requirements after dark can be minimised by a combination of smart controls and commercial wind power.

The reason this is so important is that it means we now have at our disposal a proven method to reduce the peak-electricity grid demand of our domestic and non-domestic buildings. So for the first time it makes economic sense to divert money from building expensive energy-hungry power stations and instead use the money to transform our buildings so they require very little energy from the grid.

The economic benefits include:
» Diverting money from subsidising energy companies to creating thousands of new jobs in a new green economic revolution (cost-neutral with the bonus of a reduced need for social benefits).
» Reduced expenditure on fuel imports for years to come (savings on foreign expenditure worth billions of pounds).
» Export of the products and skills of the new green economic revolution (foreign-exchange income).

With Passive design it is possible to deliver a healthy, prosperous, low-carbon future right now. This can be paid for by diverting funds from the production of energy to the saving of energy, and my experience is that the techniques to achieve this are quickly learnt.

I think that the RIBA should be giving policy-makers clear evidence from academic research that shows what works best, together with the strongest possible reassurance that architects are now ready to lead the construction industry in the transformational change that is necessary to create very low-carbon buildings.

▶ **Right:** *The Muse, Newington Green, London*

A New Kind of Suburbia

by Neil Deely

This design for rented homes is a new offer – unmatched by conventional volume house builders – of clusters of adaptable homes in a spacious, almost rural setting. Its flexibility and construction efficiency offers new advantages for both renters and institutional investors as predicted increases in households materialise.

The design provides the opportunity to flex the mix of occupancies/density within the same two-storey built

envelopes – 'dial-a-density' – ensuring that the scheme can be attuned to location-specific need/market demand and adapted over time. Our layout shows a wide range of densities between 25dph and a more sustainable 50dph and it can be adapted to suit any site size, shape or context.

Conventional suburbia maximises private space. Our design provides space in radically different ways – a neighbourhood park, communal gardens, allotments

Neil Deely
Architect
Partner, Metropolitan Workshop
www.metwork.co.uk

▼ *Below:* Houses overlook communal space and shared facilities. Metropolitan Workshop won the RIBA/Wates competition for alternative housing in the private rental market

and orchards – for recreation and biodiversity. It can also offer retail and workspaces to link with neighbouring communities, encouraging social inclusion.

Density and mix

The layout shows 25dph dwellings but density can be increased to 45dph within the same envelope with significant benefits to cost and quality. Higher densities will reduce the cost of infrastructure per home, permitting enhanced quality and higher-specification communal facilities and potentially reducing maintenance costs.

Our design could accommodate between 250 and c.500 homes – shifting to the mix the Office for National Statistics demography suggests may be required in future – in contrast with the common for-sale layouts of large family homes.

Typologies: flexible layout, adaptable plans

The same T-shaped envelope can deliver different mixes and houses can easily be adapted into maisonettes in the future. This means tenants can move within the scheme, maintaining community bonds, reducing voids and so enhancing rental income. Our T-shaped envelopes can provide either four one-bedroom flats plus one two-bedroom house; six one-bedroom maisonettes; three three-bedroom houses; or one multi-generational house.

Issues we considered:

1. Sharing and community

We envisage communities will form through incentivising longer tenancies, providing high-quality shared landscape amenities and promoting shared activities. If the management of the settlement is successful and the viability of the scheme can support a better place to live, then tenants will stay longer and the community will be stronger. We propose four kinds of shared space: neighbourhood park, street gardens, collegial courts and communal yards provide

▲ *Above: Communal yard – private terrace with view over play area/ hobby hut/shed*

very different amenities, from informal to intimate and pre-programmed to self-managed.

2. Flexibility

Our scheme offers a range of accommodation that is suitable for all stages of life and modes of living. From shared houses, popular with the young, to the bungalows and extra care desired in later years, our scheme should attract a cross-section of the future UK demography.

The variety of accommodation and the predictability of an Assured Shorthold Tenancy mean people will only have to move away if they wish to. Our dwellings are compatible with current policy on housing benefit so that if a resident's financial circumstances deteriorate they can stay put. Most dwellings are designed to share, so reconfiguration should not be the only option.

3. Viability and investors

At higher densities our efficient scheme should target the yields that institutional investors in the private rented sector (PRS) demand. Phased take-up, low-maintenance buildings and longer average lease terms will also streamline the financial equation. Phaseability by cluster will ensure that take-up is quick; low-lifecycle maintenance costs will result from robust design; slower churn and a reduction in voids will be achieved by incentivising longer tenancies. Intensified density from 25dph to 50dph will provide the critical mass necessary for management efficiencies. The scheme could be made denser by building over three floors and converting street gardens to conventional streets.

4. Landlords

The scheme will meet the needs of the companies that build and operate it by being repetitive and flexible. The envelope will remain largely constant regardless of the location-specific mix. Detailing and construction technology will be robust and simple, designed specifically for the demands of PRS and adaptable to context.

Shared housing also provides the most economic means of renting for the tenant. Compact built forms will keep energy costs down and construction and floor-space efficiencies high. Higher densities will improve viability.

5. Customers

The unique selling point of this scheme is a community

Above: Housing layout plan showing different scales of communal open space

that looks and feels like a special piece of suburbia, providing a better place to live than a volume house builder settlement. Its attractiveness would come from the trustworthiness of an institutional landlord, low energy costs, community spirit, access to well managed amenities and possibly lower rents bought by higher densities. The conviviality of the place and the purpose-built quality of the accommodation and landscapes will become a better option than London's tired suburban buy-to-let market.

The scheme also offers a type of environment that new-build owner-occupier stock does

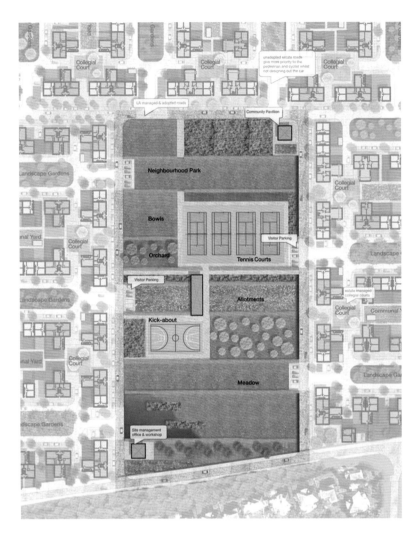

◀ **Left:** *Plans of the gardens, tennis courts, allotments, community pavilion and parking area.*

not, potentially providing more to the renter than most owner-occupiers enjoy. The amenities the place contains and the reputation it builds will make it a desirable alternative to home ownership, providing UK residents with much greater choice in how to live.

6. Context

Our scheme can easily adjust to meet particular demographic and social trends through the flexibility of its layout and the varieties of dwelling type. The ethos that underpins the place can be delivered regardless of accommodation mix. Through its design and management, the scheme will provide real opportunities for residents to develop a strong sense of belonging, creating a stable community that will promote a greater sense of shared ethos and identity.

A desirably different alternative to owner-occupier housing may help to rebalance the nation's need to own and re-establish a better sense of community stewardship. Environmentally, this compact and greened housing settlement will provide a multitude of benefits and offers a new model for green belt and suburbia to intertwine.

Wilderness City

by Bryan Avery

Bryan Avery
Architect
Avery Associates Architects
www.avery-architects.co.uk

Once upon a time there were just two very basic but deeply significant environments for mankind. There was the wilderness – that frightening, unknown, unknowable world outside; and there was the home. Be it a cave or a town, the home was the safe haven from man's fears, and for millennia the idea of a safe haven defined the town.

The security of the home-town freed its people to nurture the intellectual talents that had hitherto been a liability and thus began the long process towards a cohesive and mutually beneficial social structure, which would eventually allow a level of prosperity to develop in the towns that was impossible to imagine in the wilderness. At its simplest, the relationship between wilderness and town was symbiotic, with the town depending on the wilderness for its raw materials, and the wilderness depending on the town for its trade.

The system's death knell was the Industrial Revolution. Pastoral wealth was suddenly eclipsed by industrial wealth. The countryside was denuded of labour and new towns sprang up for industrial purposes almost entirely unconnected with the rural economy. The local interdependencies that had shaped so much of the landscape of the past were broken. Mechanised transportation and communication systems at first linked towns locally, then nationally, then globally.

While the UK has had almost 200 years to adjust to this process, in the countries of the developing world the changes have been cataclysmic.

Life in the wilderness was hard and nature was unforgiving, but people newly freed from the dawn-to-dusk tyranny of the land soon found that their age-old skills and habits were unwanted in the towns. Looking back at what they had lost, they found that the towns had taken and redefined the wilderness as a countryside in its own image.

There was now no safe haven. The deep bond between the wild places where man is not the master and the safe havens of our towns had been broken.

Thus the pressure for change began, and the whole structure of the modern town has evolved as a dynamic, never-ending system of infrastructural redevelopment. With this comes upheaval, danger and a dependency on urban systems we cannot comprehend and which are as uncertain as the vagaries of nature we left the wilderness to escape. Nevertheless, we must accept that our towns will in the future become very much denser than today because land is a finite commodity and we must use it sparingly.

We should start by restraining out towns, not by 'green belts' that can be easily breached, but by a physical barrier – new town walls. Almost all of the world's most cherished urban environments have been constrained in some way, usually by geography or by man-made defensive walls.

The 'walls' in this case would be raised roads, viaducts, which would contain below them shopping and commercial districts, placed back-to-back perhaps with housing. These walls are thus permeable to pedestrians at ground level, and to maximise development potential the perimeter of each cell would be built to the highest densities. This would free the centre to become the cultural and socio-political heart of the community, with spaces that would be tranquil and of public scale.

Within the walls residents would be obliged to be inventive in order to increase density. When this was exhausted, new autonomous townships would be founded, each separated from its neighbour by landscaped public parkland open to all. Such townships could have their own economic structures and would thus have their own identities and characters. If the cells of such a city could be made as desirable as a

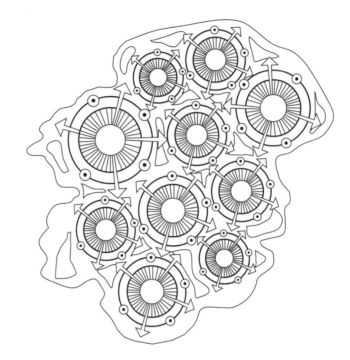

small market town in scale and character, it would release pressure on the countryside, which could then revert to its original state as the necessary wilderness in counterpoint to the town. Thus the symbiotic relationship between the two would be restored.

▲ *Above:* Township cells coalescing into a city

▼ *Below:* Two hamlet cells

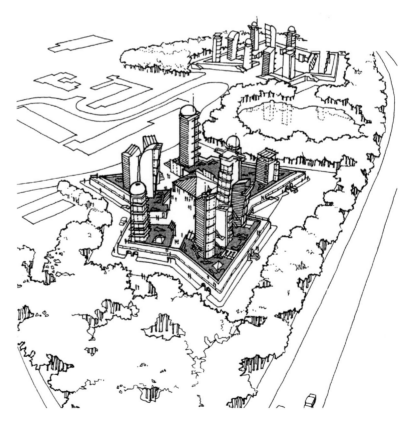

So Watt About China: the Power of 7 Billion Watts. (What's...? What, Me?)

by David Hampton

David Hampton
Carbon Coach
Chartered Environmentalist
www.socenv.org.uk

I've been advising individuals on their ecological footprint for nine years now, as a 'carbon coach' – think personal trainer, nutritionist, lifestyle motivator. Before that I was a sustainability consultant, advising professionals and governments on award-winning projects. Often these were just slightly less damaging variants of 'business as usual'.

I was frequently invited to speak about the climate crisis. Few people were talking about the funny weather back then, but the gathering purple storm cloud was bothering me deeply. Whenever anyone dared speak of carbon emissions, the usual retort was: 'Ah, but what about China?' As if that ended the matter.

Here's how I used to answer: 'Do you know that a Chinese person has an overall carbon footprint ONE QUARTER the size of that of a person in the US? And half the size of that of a person in the UK? Plus, they make most of our stuff and deal with most of our waste. Now, remind me, what was your question about China?'

As for me? I've never been to China. Most carbon coaches don't fly. But I have made up for my lack of first-hand experience, and avoided the need to travel, by doing the maths. In the UK roughly every £150 we save on gas or every £300 we save on electricity, every £600 we save on petrol or every six hours we avoid flying, equals one ton of CO_2e not released into the atmosphere. Each of these items saves a ton, 1000kg, on our personal greenhouse-gas tally. The fuel sums will be different for China, but the one ton of CO_2e for every six hours in the air is a vital, and little known, universal rule: 'I will, even if you won't.'

In 2000 I attended a course on business and sustainability at Schumacher College. It changed my life. I got Gaia'd, as it's affectionately called. Roughly translated, that's a bodily experience of deep ecology, a reconnection with nature. After returning to the college three more times, I paused to work out what needed to happen next. Eureka! Reduce my footprint! So that is what I did.

Looking back, I can see what was happening. Each guru, each teacher, each thought-leader, was audaciously expounding what needed to happen next, globally. Certainly none of them professed to overlook the vital importance of leading from the front, but their intellects, capabilities and giant visions were not to be stifled by any worthy focus on their own carbon footprints.

We assumed we were all wiping our own carbon boots. We were busy seeking far-off solutions instead of leading attractive, infectious, low-carbon lifestyles, here and now, ourselves. If we had to fly to China once a week to implement global sustainability visions… we'd do it!

'In theory, practice and theory are the same. In practice they are not.' Some of the papers here rightly look at the gap between design and delivery. But there's a much bigger gap ahead, one we cannot imagine. There's a perfect global storm of economic, climate, resource, political and social bubbles all set to burst over the next decade or so. These can be delayed, but not avoided.

After this shake-out, truly sustainable lifestyles will arise again, naturally, green shoots and grass roots, all over China and elsewhere. They will be unplanned and unplannable.

The human impulse for the miracle of life will prevail.

New lifestyles will be locally inspired. They will be ultra-low or no-impact. Mother Nature, not human Grand Designs, will resume charge as Global Masterplanner. Radically different, sustainable lifestyles will naturally emerge – just not the ones we currently imagine or carelessly wish for.

The people of China will take responsibility and vote with their feet. If they believe now that what they really need is more roads, for example, those roads could be designed to be readily 'up-cycled' and reclaimed as cycle paths or even allotments.

In the new reality, people will make creative ecological use of whatever construction legacy we now think to impose. They will work out how to live, eat, travel and to cluster. We can't foresee this because the

▲ *Above:* *Imagining fair shares of carbon with pupils of Downsell Primary School in Leyton*

gap between what we think people may want tomorrow and what the people will really need tomorrow is too vast. All we can do is pave the way for highly creative ecological human inventiveness, born of necessity.

We can design for radical, local self-transformation. We are learning the importance of 'slow' for sustainable living: slow design, slow burn, slow travel, slow food. We would be wise not to superimpose or indelibly imprint 'fast' onto a global village that is about to rediscover the joy of slow.

As the Brundtland Commission (almost) says: 'Development that inherently enables future generations to meet their basic human needs, without too badly compromising our ability to carry on unsustainably for just a short while longer.'

City of Shallow Hollows

by Owen O'Carroll

Owen O'Carroll
Architect
Director of UrbanX

What role or responsibility does the west have in contributing to the positive evolution of the new cities of the east?

China's rapidly evolving urban environment presents a laboratory for change in the east and poses questions about urban transformation in the west. Its increasing reproduction of western urban and architectural models, embedding meanings and messages so different historically to the urban reality of the east, is a cause of great concern.

China's increasing aspiration for (individual) economic independence as a means to secure the mass transformation of the nation finds a key model in 21st-century 'modernism'. With cities increasing in scale, the failures and faults of modernism become more clear. Do we, who clearly understand modernism's history and language, have any responsibility for society's urban outcomes? How terrifying to see the east reconstructing and re-interpreting failed models as new symbols for an eastern audience.

'Trophy' designers imported to 'redefine' quality only exacerbate a misunderstanding of 'modernism'. Is this no more than another, cynical, reinterpretation of the consultancy and professionalism sold to the 'new' middle east, now recurring again in China?

Same difference

China is different in so many ways to the west – yet we share characteristics and hopes, problems and needs. Historically the Chinese city is based on the principles of *Kao Gong Ji* ('The Records of Works', a chapter of the *Zhouli* or 'Rites of the Zhou Empire') embedded as a set of urban and design guidelines for city growth. Basic city structure and layout were governed; prime highways were both roadways and waterways; there was a cellurised urban system of districts and urban units; and the 'wall' was a fundamental urban and architectural device, defining productive

▼ *Below:* 'East Meets West', *Philip Rhys Matthews*

and residential space and shaping communities and city space. Public space traditionally relied simply on the shared space of the street, with crossroads and nodes as the key points of interaction and transaction. Any large public spaces served as spaces of separation, providing protection typically to palaces or administrative centres. By contrast, the modernism of the 20th century presented a new political vision through space, architecture, openness and, importantly, choice.

Following the Xinhai Revolution of 1911, in parallel with the evolution of the 'Ville Radieuse', China imported 1920s Beaux-Arts approaches, followed by Clarence Perry's US 'Neighbourhood Unit' as a key planning and urban form. Following the end of the Sino-Japanese war in 1945, the cold war brought 10,000 Russian planners. The 'superblock' became the new modernism – high rise, economic, spatially intense, a new, highly technical means to organise planned residential areas, distribute urban services effectively, prevent the devaluation of real estate and stop the development of slums. Ironically, the earlier mid-rise neigbourhood unit was now considered bourgeois.

The work unit and beyond
New economies grew around the 'work unit', the place of production. Even today, almost 90 per cent of public housing is owned and controlled by work units, which represent both 'family' and 'authority'. 'Family' encapsulated a way of life, a trade, a profession,

a relationship; 'authority' brought social and community services, devolved by the state, bestowing ownership and decision-making about the city on the unit. The 'wall' re-engaged with the new urban form, visibly defining the work unit's extent and world.

The drive towards capitalisation and matching western living standards allowed both work unit and superblock to drive city expansion and evolution. The development of a new private sector with an economic independence at both individual and corporate level further opened up demand for new urban models. Thus began the next wave of city building – importing, rebuilding and re-interpreting western urban and architectural typologies. New islands of desire and trophies of acquisition were created, counterpoints to the historic models of neighbourhood units and the traditional city.

The 21st-century recalibration of values from a collective responsibility and contribution to an individual one is seismic for China. The ability now to live the 'western life' drives the new urban culture.

A new 21st-century urbanism
Historically the Chinese city has not needed the notions and forms of western public space, yet the new culture of independence and individuality needs physically to reflect the interactivity, connectivity, coincidence and surprise of the digital world (the world without walls) that is already so greatly inhabited by China. Places

of transaction, interaction and reaction, so important culturally, educationally and economically, are missing from the current modernist 'notion' of the Chinese city. Ironically, we see a modernist urbanism and architecture still separated by the 'wall' – except now the wall is the 'highway', the flyover, the piecemeal fractured development of urban islands – a pattern of disconnection. So what is the implication for the west?

We too have the same patterns and problems, dysfunctional modernisms, failed values and aspirations, protected and reprotected boundaries. How do we renew and repair them at an urban level? Do we in the west, as originators of this language, have a responsibility to the east? Should we take an active part in repairing our mistakes within emerging economies?

It's clear we have a responsibility: we cannot recycle past thinking and projects and then abandon the territory simply because we claim 'no ownership'. The opportunities and pitfalls of modernist planning and design lie more at our door than at the east's. We are the 'elder brother'. We have more to gain, and more to lose. Cities are easier to build than to transform or tear down.

Chinese cities used to be referred to as 'Cities of Shallow Hollows', a benign reference to their scale and internal openness. How should we refer to them now – as 'Cities of Modernisms', perhaps?

Image credits

1	Dr Jihad Awad, Ajman
2	Agnes Sanvito NLA
5 (top)	Peter Head
5 (middle, bottom)	Laura Lee
6/7, 9 (top)	Arup
9 (bottom)	The Ecological Sequestration Trust
11 (top)	Daniel Hambury
11 (bottom)	Philipp Rode
12	Phil Sayer
13, 14	Rogers Stirk Harbour + Partners
15, 16, 17	Farrells
18	Hufton & Crow
19, 20	Transport for London
21, 22	London Legacy Development Corporation
23 (top)	Design Council
23 (bottom), 24	Design Council; photographer – Ed Sykes
25	English Heritage
26 (left and top)	Mark Irving, Berwick upon Tweed
26 (bottom)	English Heritage/Derek Kendall
27, 28, 29, 30	The Academy of Urbanism
31, 32, 33	Ken Yeang (2015)
35, 36	Zedfactory
37, 38	Wilkinson Eyre
39 (top)	NSE Architects

39 (middle and bottom), 40 (top)	Arshak Katchryan/NSE Architects
40 (bottom)	Nigel Eckersall/Arshak Katchryan
41 (top)	James Jordan
41 (bottom), 42 (top), 43, 44	Angela Brady
42 (bottom)	Brady Mallalieu Architects
45, 46	Bohn&Viljoen
47 (top)	Rory Buckland
47 (bottom)	Red Carnation Hotels
48 (top)	Angela Brady
48 (bottom)	Michael Murray
49 (top)	Professor Roland Ennos
49 (middle)	Angela Brady
49 (bottom)	A R Ennos (2010); Urban Cool, Physics World 23 (8), 22-25, reprinted with permission
51 (top)	Sue James
51 (bottom)	Trees and Design Action Group
53 (top), 54, 55	Sue Roaf
53 (bottom)	Image courtesy of NASA/ Goddard Space Flight Center Scientific Visualization Studio
57	Alan Penn
59	Judit Kimpian
60	AHR
61, 62	John Thompson & Partners
63 (top), 64	David Twohig
63 (bottom)	Jason Clarke Photography

65 (top)	Simon Warren
65 (bottom), 68	Cullinan Studio
66-67	Hayes Davidson
69	BuroHappold
70	1MDB
71, 72	Sturgis Carbon Profiling
73 (top)	Micha Theiner
73 (bottom)	Tim Crocker
74	Jefferson Smith
75, 76, 77, 78	Metwork
79, 80	Bryan Avery
81	Christopher Anton
82	David Hampton and Diana Korchien
83 (top)	Morley von Sternberg
84 (bottom)	Philip Rhys Matthews
Back cover	Angela Brady